D0880834

The Italian Shakespearians

Other Books by Marvin Carlson

André Antoine's Memories of the Théâtre-Libre (1964)
The Theatre of the French Revolution (1966)
The French Stage in the Nineteenth Century (1972)
The German Stage in the Nineteenth Century (1972)
Goethe and the Weimar Theatre (1978)
The Italian Stage from Goldoni to D'Annunzio (1981)
Theories of the Theatre (1984)

The Italian Shakespearians

Performances by Ristori, Salvini, and Rossi
in England and America

Marvin Carlson

Folger Books
Washington: The Folger Shakespeare Library
London and Toronto: Associated University Presses

© 1985 by Associated University Presses, Inc.

Associated University Presses
440 Forsgate Drive
Cranbury, NJ 08512

Associated University Presses
25 Sicilian Avenue
London WC1A 2QH, England

Associated University Presses
2133 Royal Windsor Drive
Unit 1
Mississauga, Ontario
Canada L5J 1K5

Library of Congress Cataloging in Publication Data

Carlson, Marvin A., 1935–
    The Italian Shakespearians.

    Bibliography: p.
    Includes index.
    1. Shakespeare, William, 1564–1616—Stage history—
1800–1950.   2. Shakespeare, William, 1564–1616—Stage
history—United States.   3. Ristori, Adelaide, 1822–1906.
4. Salvini, Tommaso, 1829–1916.   5. Rossi, Ernesto,
1827–1896.   6. Actors—Italy—Biography.   7. Acting—
History.   8. Theater—England—History—19th century.
9. Theater—United States—History—19th century.
I. Title.
PR3112.C37   1985   792.9′5   84-48131
ISBN 0-918016-76-2 (alk. paper)

Printed in the United States of America

Contents

Salvini as Othello (Folger Shakespeare Library)

Acknowledgments

To Eric Salmon and the University of Guelph, who in 1976 organized a delightful conference on Sarah Bernhardt. The paper I presented there on the American tours of Ristori and the stimulating discussions on the phenomenon of the international star provided the germ of the present book. The paper was published, in slightly modified form, in Salmon's *Sarah Bernhardt and the Theatre of Her Time* (Greenwood, 1983), and it provided some material for the American section of part 2 of the present study.

To Cornell University and Dean Alain Seznec for arranging an administrative leave that provided time for research.

To the archivists and librarians of the Cornell University Library, the Library of Congress, the Folger Shakespeare Library, the Performing Arts Collection of the New York Public Library, and the Lilly Library at Indiana University who aided in the finding of material and especially in the tracing of itineraries.

To the Departments of Theatre at Cornell University and at Ohio State Universities for inviting me to participate in, respectively, a *Hamlet* Conference in the Spring of 1979 and a *King Lear* Conference the following Spring. Presenting and discussing the performances of Salvini and Rossi in these contexts was extremely helpful in focusing upon the special quality of their interpretations and of the Italian style as opposed to other nineteenth-century approaches.

To L. W. Conolly for inviting me to submit an essay on Rossi in
America for his anthology *Theatrical Touring and Founding in
North America* (Greenwood, 1982). Like the earlier Ristori
essay, this on Rossi provided an opportunity to draw together a variety of material on Italian touring in America,
and chapter 10 of the present book utilizes, in its sections
on performances in America, some of this same research.

To the Burcado Archives in Rome, the Harvard University Library, and the Folger Shakespeare Library in Washington
for their kind permission to reproduce material from their
collections.

All translations, unless otherwise noted, are my own.

The Italian Shakespearians

1

Shakespeare Comes to Italy

One of the most striking manifestations of the late nineteenth-century theatre was the international star. Without regard for the old barriers of language or cultural tradition, these remarkable actors and actresses roamed throughout Europe and in time to America and Asia as well, dazzling the theatre-going public wherever they went. Italy, despite the comparative weakness of its own dramatic tradition, carried off most of the honors of this era of international touring, beginning with Ristori, continuing with Salvini and Rossi, and ending the century with Duse. Although the touring Italian stars naturally offered plays of their homeland, a major part of their repertoire, taken as a whole, was devoted to Shakespeare, and several of them gained their greatest success in Shakespearian roles. Thus, when they toured to England and to the United States, audiences were offered the unusual experience of witnessing their most familiar playwright being presented not only by an actor from an alien tradition, but one speaking another tongue. The many eyewitness accounts of these popular performances provide a revealing record of what these foreign interpretations looked like to English-speaking audiences and what new values and insights they offered.

Despite Shakespeare's fascination with Italy as a locale for his plays, the Italian knowledge of the English dramatist developed very slowly. When Apostolo Zeno produced a music drama named *Ambleto* in 1705 he was apparently quite unaware that a significant English drama had been created on the same subject a century before. The first known mention of the English dramatist by an Italian comes from a letter written in 1715 and published in 1726 by the Paduan poet and man of letters Antonio Conti, who visited London between 1715 and 1718 and encountered Shakespearian drama there. Under its inspiration he began his own *Giulio Cesare*, which owed to Shakespeare at most its subject, for all of Conti's works were scrupulously faithful to the precepts of French neoclassicism. The letter, published as a preface to *Giulio Cesare*, noted that "Sasper is the Corneille of the English, only far more irregular," treating "Aristotle's rules with contempt." It is unfortunate, Conti feels, that this English dramatist was unknown in Italy in the seventeenth century, when the Italians, "spoilt by Spanish comedies," would have responded favorably to such crude but vigorous work.[1]

Conti's comparison and frame of reference are highly revealing, for all through the eighteenth century Italy was dominated, culturally and intellectually, by France. Italian critical interest in Shakespeare thus necessarily had to wait upon the development of French critical interest, and the writings of Voltaire, which may be taken as the launching point of Shakespeare in France, served precisely the same function in Italy. Francesco Saverio Quadrio's *Della Storia e della Ragione d'Ogni Poesia* (1743) draws most of its observations directly from Voltaire's *Lettres Philosophiques* (1734), and echoes the French critic in calling Shakespeare a "fertile and vigorous genius" whose mind "combined the natural with the sublime," but whose ignorance of the rules of drama made even his virtues pernicious, since these encouraged later English dramatists to copy both his excellences and his considerable faults.[2]

The Shakespeare that the Italians became acquainted with through Voltaire was an undisciplined, erratic, even gross genius, the product of a barbaric age. They were, moreover, assured by Voltaire that the neoclassic dramas of their own culture were distinctly superior to the works of Shakespeare, despite his occasional flashes of brilliance. The preface to Voltaire's *Mérope* (1743) spoke slightingly of English drama while likening Scipione Maffei to Sophocles, and the preface to *Sémiramis* (1748), addressed to the Italian Voltarian Cardinal

Querini, called the works of Metastasio the nearest modern art had come to Greek tragedy, both in regard for the rules and in poetic achievement. This same preface contains Voltaire's famous denunciation of *Hamlet* as a "gross and barbarous piece which would not be supported by the most vile public in France and Italy" and of Shakespeare as an artist in whom nature had combined "whatever one can imagine that is most powerful and good" with "the lowest and most detestable elements of an uninspired grossness."[3]

Observations such as these made Italian men of letters aware of Shakespeare but gave them little encouragement to read him. The English stage, as Voltaire had pointed out, showed the danger of contamination from too close an acquaintance with this undisciplined barbarian. Goldoni provides an excellent illustration of this attitude in his 1754 comedy *I Malcontenti*, created during his bitter literary dispute with the rival playwright Pietro Chiari. Chiari, parodied so openly and sarcastically in the character Grisologo that the play was banned in Venice, boasts of his study of "the celebrated Sachespir." He thus describes what he has learned from the English dramatist:

> My style, which shall make me world famous, consists in the power to speak in a vibrant, ample, sonorous manner, full of metaphors, of similes, of sententiae, which now elevate me among the stars, now bring me to skim into contact with the base earth. I am no slave to the burdensome laws of the unities. I blend tragedy with comedy, and when I write in verse I abandon myself entirely to the poetic fancy, with no regard for nature, which others obey with excessive scruple.[4]

Perhaps this caricature did not in fact represent Goldoni's true feelings about Shakespeare, or perhaps further exposure and further thought altered his opinion. In any case a very different view is expressed in a preface to this play written two years later and addressed to John Murry, the English Resident in Venice. Here Goldoni holds up the English dramatist as a "model to anyone" desiring to learn playwriting. He has shown how to escape the "cramping fetters" of Aristotle and Horace by creating dramas which are "rational imitations of human actions." As for the character Grisologo in his *Malcon-*

tenti, he is to be condemned not for attempting to follow Shakespeare but for doing so "without having first thoroughly studied him, and without those principles of nature which are necessary to drama." Therefore Grisologo has achieved "only a ridiculous caricature."[5]

A much more open champion of Shakespeare soon appeared in Giuseppe Baretti, who returned to Venice in 1762 after a ten-year sojourn in England and founded a journal, the *Frusta letteraria,* modelled on the English *Rambler.* Here he assailed the neoclassic academies, the French, and such literary lights as Goldoni and Chiari, both of whom he considered servile imitators of the French style. French rules, he argued, might be suitable for France, but were irrelevant across the channel or beyond the Alps, where could be found "transcendental poets" such as Ariosto or Shakespeare, "whose genius soars beyond the reach of art." Shakespeare "in both comedy and tragedy supasses all the Corneilles, Racines, and Molières of Gaul."[6]

Baretti's defiant tone did not win many Italian converts to Shakespeare. On the contrary, his journal stirred up so much opposition that it was supressed by the Venetian authorities and Baretti felt obliged to return to London in 1766. There in a series of writings during the 1760s and 1770s he continued his championship of Shakespeare and of the Spanish Renaissance dramatists against the attacks of the neoclassics, and especially of Voltaire, whose attitude toward the English dramatist became increasingly intolerant as the century progressed and as Shakespeare began to have more French disciples. The most famous of Voltaire's anti-Shakespearian tracts, the 1776 *Discours* to the French Academy, inspired Baretti's most extended defense of Shakespeare, the 1777 *Discours sur Shakespeare et sur Monsieur de Voltaire,* a striking preromantic manifesto, which declared "Let Aristotle say what he will, I oppose to his authority the experience of Shakespeare, of Lope de Vega, and of several others, who have made us see the contrary."[7]

Baretti's article, written in French and published in Paris, where it gained little attention, was, not surprisingly, little noticed in Italy. In August, 1778, Baretti wrote to a friend in Milan, which was now emerging as the new literary capital of Italy: "You are deceived if you believe that I had hoped my friends in Milan would approve of my debate with M. de Voltaire. I know the present world well enough not to flatter myself in regard to their approval. But I have not written for the present world. I write primarily for the future."[8] Indeed the coming romantic movement would, within a generation, fully vindicate Baretti's position.

The first attempts to stage Shakespeare in Italy were made near the end of the century, but hardly in a form Baretti would countenance. A version of *Hamlet* enjoyed a respectable run of nine nights at the San Giovanni Grisostomo theatre in Venice and was successfully revived in Bologna and elsewhere. It was based, however, upon the French adaptation by Jean François Ducis, who had totally regularized the play according to eighteenth-century taste. The cast was reduced to eight, several of them confidantes, the unities were rigidly followed, and Ophelia was made the daughter of Claudius, so that the plot could hinge upon the Corneillian dilemma of Hamlet being forced to choose between his love and his duty.[9] A similar success was gained a few years later by a similarly corrupted *Romeo and Juliet*, drawn from the French adaptation of Mercier which observed the unities, changed the tone from tragedy to sentimental comedy, and ended happily with a reconciliation of the feuding families and uniting of the young lovers. Even so, Vincenzo Monti, the leading Italian tragedian at the turn of the century, admitted in a 1789 preface to shedding tears "over the adventures of Romeo and Juliet" and leaving the theatre "struck with terror and horror by the fury of Hamlet."[10]

The first attempt to present a more honest version of Shakespeare on the Italian stage was made by the leading actor of serious drama in late eighteenth-century Italy, Antonio Morrocchesi. Morrocchesi had already built a major reputation as an interpreter of the tragedies of Vittorio Alfieri when in 1793 he appeared in a series of benefit performances at Florence's Teatro di Borgognissanti. Alfieri's *Mirra* and *Oreste* were offered on the first and third evenings, and between them *Amleto, Principe di Danimarca*, translated by Alessandro Verri. A two-month visit to England in 1767 had inspired Verri to translate both *Othello* and *Hamlet* in moderately faithful though plodding versions which had never yet seen the stage. Clearly Morrocchesi was uneasy about the reception of this new drama, because in the Alfieri works he appeared under his own name, but in *Amleto* as Alessio Zaccagnini. His caution appeared justified. The audience found Verri's lame verses and Shakespeare's carelessness about neoclassic rules uninteresting and even irritating and received the experiment very badly.[11] *Amleto* was not offered again, and for more than a quarter of a century after this isolated experiment, Shakespeare was represented on the Italian stage only by such adaptations as gave no suggestion whatever of the original—operas, ballets, and neoclassic reworkings in the manner of Ducis.

The leading tragedians of this period in Italy—Alfieri and subsequently Monti, Ugo Foscolo, and Giovanni Pindemonte—all expressed warm praise for the English dramatist, but in theory and practice remained far closer to Voltaire. Alfieri lists Shakespeare along with Racine and Aeschylus in his *Vita* as one of the dramatists he most reveres, but like Voltaire he finds a danger in this very attraction: "However much I felt myself drawn toward this author (all of whose defects at the same time I could very well see), I was that much more determined to keep away from him."[12] Similarly Foscolo in a letter of 1809 rhetorically inquired who did not feel his mind broadened and elevated by reading the "sublime" Shakespeare but went on to inquire who at the same time was unaware of the faults and extravagances of this author.[13]

Only one dramatist of this period, the rather eccentric Count Alessandro Pepoli, openly broke with neoclassicism in the name of Shakespeare, issuing a sort of preromantic manifesto in the *Mercurio d'Italia* in 1796 entitled "On the usefulness, the invention, and the rules of a new type of theatrical composition, called a 'fisedia.' " The Shakespearian *fisedia* rejected unity of time and place, allowed the use of both kings and peasants, mixed comic and tragic elements, and used both prose and verse. Its only rules, said Pepoli, were those "followed by all worthwhile plays," such as "consistency of character, propriety of manners, and clarity of development."[14] His *Ladislo*, created according to these precepts, enjoyed a modest success in Venice in 1796, but did not inspire any significant followers. The influence of the French tradition, reinforced by the growing influence of Alfierian neoclassicism, proved too strong for this alien form to overcome.

The coming of romanticism naturally brought with it fresh interest in Shakespeare, who was regarded by romantic theorists throughout Europe as the model for their revolt against neoclassic theatre. The romantic movement in Italy is generally considered to have begun with the publication in January, 1816, in Milan of Mme. de Staël's "Sulla maniera e la utilità della traduzioni," which condemned the vapidity of contemporary Italian literature and urged young Italian writers to turn to Shakespeare as well as to other English and German authors as new models for inspiration. A heated debate over this advice followed in the literary circles of Milan, but many young authors were indeed stimulated by Mme. de Staël's challenge. Alessandro Manzoni, who became the leading Italian romantic writer, informed a friend in France in a letter of March, 1816, that he had undertaken his first drama, a verse tragedy called *Il Conte di Carmagnola*, under the influence of "Shakespeare and some things recently written about the theatre."[15]

At this same time Michele Leoni in Florence undertook the ambitious project suggested by Mme. de Staël, a complete translation of Shakespeare, publishing fourteen plays, most of them in verse, between 1819 and 1822. Although the plays were accompanied by prefaces translated from A. W. Schlegel, the leading German romanticist, Leoni was still unwilling to depart too radically from neoclassic practice. *Otello*, the first of these new translations to reach the stage, followed the traditional unities and much simplified the action, reducing the characters to only Othello, Cassio, Iago, Desdemona, and Roderigo. The actor who first performed this adaptation (in Naples in 1820) was Francesco Lombardi. Like Morrocchesi he had gained his reputation in the tragedies of Alfieri, but Lombardi was a leader in the new romantic style of acting, erratic and emotional, rather in the manner of Edmund Kean in England. Lombardi revived this role from time to time, but it was never apparently considered among his best. There is little evidence that audiences were interested in the drama itself; the main attraction was clearly Lombardi's violent and sensational acting. His epileptic seizure was considered the high point of the interpretation.[16]

By 1830 romanticism had triumphed in Italian letters and

Shakespeare, at least in literary circles, was accepted without qualification as a major poet. Manzoni, whose praise for the English dramatist was frequent and enthusiastic, had replaced Voltaire as the spokesman for the Italian literary consciousness. Between 1829 and 1831 twelve new Shakespearian translations were published, by six different translators, and were widely read and discussed. Still, this growing interest did not greatly affect the general public, and for many years no actor followed Lombardi in the staging of any Shakespearian works. The wisdom of this caution was shown in 1842 when the leading actor of the new generation, Gustavo Modena, was tempted to continue the experimentation of Lombardi and Morrocchesi. He first considered offering *Hamlet* for a benefit performance in Turin, which would have been the first Italian attempt at this play since Morrocchesi's half a century before, but after a series of catastrophic rehearsals and many sleepless nights, Modena renounced the idea at the last minute and presented instead Voltaire's *Mahomet*, a proven success.

He next considered *Othello*, which, at least in Lombardi's interpretation, had enjoyed a modest success in the preceding generation. The Leoni translation was used as a base, but Modena adjusted many parts of it to bring it as close to Shakespeare as he felt contemporary taste would accept. Endless pains were taken with the staging; once again rehearsals were long and difficult and the actors, including Modena himself, approached the opening with the greatest trepidation. Several years later Modena described to his student Rossi the catastrophic opening of this production at Milan's Teatro Re. As soon as Roderigo began to shout for Brabantio the audience began to whisper: "What is it? A tragedy or a farce?" When Brabantio appeared on the balcony half asleep and with his clothing disordered he was greeted by laughter, then by hisses and whistles. The curtain was lowered and the performance ended, according to Modena, before he even made an appearance on stage.[17]

Notices in the Milan journals of the period tell a rather different story, and one rather less flattering to the actor. According to them the play was given a complete hearing, but despite the efforts of its star was received by its audience with complete indifference.[18] In any case, Modena was sufficiently discouraged not to attempt Shakespeare again. The dramatist was not, however, so far from success on the Italian stage as this ill-fated *Othello* would suggest. Among the young actors trained by Modena were those who would gain some of their most resounding successes in Shakespearian roles not only in Italy, but around the world. In the meantime, new and more faithful translations continued to appear. In 1839 Carlo Rusconi published a two-volume prose translation far more accurate than Leoni's, and his *Macbeth* and *Hamlet* (with a happy ending) were presented with moderate success in Milan and other cities in the early 1850s by one of Modena's protégés, Alemanno Morelli.[19] The critic Pietro Ferrigni later wrote that Morelli was "unsurpassed in the intelligence" of the "diverse and protean" Hamlet, "so tormented and so unlike our own tradition. He invested Hamlet with all the majesty of his misfortune; and in moments of delirium and hallucination revealed with glance, gesture, and tone of voice the internal struggle between his fear of revealing the truth and his disgust at seeing the lie triumph."[20]

The repetition of this production for several evenings suggested that public opinion was beginning to shift to accomodate Shakespearian drama. The definitive triumph of that drama lay just ahead and was achieved almost simultaneously by two other pupils of Modena—Ernesto Rossi and Tommaso Salvini. Rossi seems to have been the first attracted to Shakespeare, expressing an interest in the work of the English dramatist soon after joining Modena's company in 1846. Modena gave him his own copies of *Hamlet* and *Othello*, but warned him that his own experience in Milan just three years before had convinced him that the Italian public was far from ready for such works. Rossi, undeterred, began seeking better translations than those by Leoni which Modena had given him. He read the French versions of Ducis and others and found them totally unacceptable. The Rusconi translations were now available and Rossi found this *Hamlet* attractive, but *Othello*, the other play which most interested him, he felt could not, as a less philosophical and more emotional work, be rendered in prose.

Fortunately a new set of translations in poetic form was now appearing, the work of Giulio Carcano. Carcano's interest in Shakespeare was stimulated by the enthusiam of Manzoni and other romantics, and like Rossi he felt that the prose approach of Rusconi captured little of Shakespeare's power. He therefore attempted a poetic rendition of a few scenes of *King Lear* in a book of poems published in 1839. These attracted the attention and the praise of many literary figures, among them Giovan Battista Niccolini, the leading serious dramatist of the period, and Carcano was encouraged to translate the complete play by 1843. A *Lettera sul dramma* prefacing this translation credited Italy with the rediscovery of tragedy "at a time when in the rest of Europe the populace still flocked to those odd and monstrous parodies called mysteries," but that soon after this discovery, the initiative shifted from Italy to England, where Shakespeare "saw in tragedy what it could be at this time, the most powerful revelation of our individuality, the representation of humanity itself in action," making him "in a certain sense the poet presaging modern Europe."[21]

After *Lear*, Carcano translated *Hamlet, Julius Caesar, Romeo and Juliet*, and *Macbeth*, the last appearing only a few days before the 1848 uprising against Austrian rule in Milan. When Austrian power was reasserted in the city, Carcano, involved in the republican cause, went into exile in Switzerland. There he was contacted by Rossi, who had organized his own company after the breakup of Modena's troupe during the upheavals of 1848. Rossi commissioned Carcano to translate *Othello*, promising him a production as soon as it was completed. The translation was completed by 1852 when Carcano returned to Milan, but by then Rossi was unable to fulfill his promise. His own company had dissolved and he had accepted the position of leading actor of the royal company in Turin. It was an excellent position for him, since the Reale Sarda was then and had been for a number of years Italy's foremost company, but Rossi was now no longer his own master and the directors of the Reale Sarda had no interest in his Shakespearian projects.

In 1855 the Reale Sarda company, headed by Rossi and

Adelaide Ristori, toured to Paris, and in 1856 to Paris and London, achieving an unprecedented international success. The triumph of Ristori, especially in the challenge which she mounted to her French rival Rachel, dominated these tours and launched Ristori on her international career. Rossi was also warmly received, but for him the major effect of the tours was surely the reinforcement which they provided for his interest in Shakespeare. In Paris he saw Wallack's troupe, also on tour, present several Shakespearian plays at the Salle Ventadour, and in London he observed Charles Kean, became friends with that actor, and brought back to Italy Kean's stage versions of *Hamlet* and *Othello* for study.[22]

In the spring of 1856, once again director of his own company and in possession of translations in which he had confidence, Rossi offered *Othello* in Milan's Teatro Re, the location of Modena's failure fourteen years before. Fourteen days later *Hamlet* was offered. Some progress had been made since the Modena experiment. At least part of the public, Rossi notes in his memoirs, were now acquainted with this style of drama and ready to accept it, and if the majority did not yet "comprehend its power and grandeur," they at least "felt that something great was to be found in it."[23] From this time onward, these and the other major Shakespearian tragedies remained the basis of Rossi's repertoire, to steadily growing public enthusiasm. He became the first Italian actor to be associated primarily with Shakespeare.

The public attention drawn by Rossi to *Hamlet* and *Othello* was reinforced by the almost simultaneous performances of the same plays by Tommaso Salvini, the other outstanding actor of the period. Salvini had been a member of Modena's troupe of youthful actors before Rossi and may have participated in the ill-received *Othello*, but if so, his autobiography does not mention it. He merely observes that until the early 1850s "the dubious outcome of several meritorious artists" who had attempted Shakespeare "dissuaded me from occupying myself overmuch with his plays."[24] In the meantime he built a substantial reputation on a largely Italian repertoire, particularly featuring the tragedies of Alfieri.

As his fame grew, Salvini became dissatisfied with the continuing demands of mounting new productions with such frequency that he rarely felt adequately prepared for a role. Accordingly, he retired from the stage for a year in 1853 to study his art and to prepare three roles in depth. The appearance of the new translations by Carcano stimulated him as they had Rossi, and *Othello* was one of the three plays he selected for study during his year of retreat. He first offered this play for a benefit in Vicenza in June of 1856, shortly after Rossi's Shakespearian productions in Milan. The public was not enthusiastic, but at least they accepted the work with mild applause and, with this modest encouragement, Salvini offered the play again for benefits in Venice and Rome. There were some complaints about its irregularity of tone and form, but Salvini was popular enough to draw audiences even for an unconventional role. *Othello* was gradually accepted, and after a few seasons even demanded. Salvini soon followed it, first in Venice, then in Florence and Rome, with a less popular but still generally praised *Hamlet*.

These first triumphs won, Shakespeare, particularly in the productions of Rossi and Salvini and in the translations of Carcano, rapidly became a significant figure on the Italian stage. By 1870 *King Lear* had been given by both actors, *Macbeth* had been given not only by these actors but by Morelli and Ristori as well, and Rossi had also offered *The Merchant of Venice, Romeo and Juliet, Coriolanus, Julius Caesar, and Richard III.* But during the years in which Shakespeare was becoming established in the Italian theatre, the same actors who had launched him there became involved in a far more vast and ambitious project— traveling throughout the world to share their vision of Shakespeare with audiences in other nations. The age of the international star had come. No nation produced a more glittering roster of these spectacular performers than Italy, and Shakespeare provided a critical part of their repertoire. Shakespeare in Italian was no longer an Italian concern but an international phenomenon, and naturally a particularly intriguing one in the English-speaking countries. It might be expected that the Italian stars would have avoided performing Shakespeare in Italian in London or New York, but on the contrary, their interest in the English dramatist appears to have encouraged them to take up this challenge, with what success we shall observe. The first star to tour outside Italy with Shakespeare, indeed the star who in many ways established the pattern for all those international tours which added so much to the brilliance of the late nineteenth-century theatre, was Adelaide Ristori.

2
The Tours of Adelaide Ristori

The idea of international theatre tours is an old one in Europe. English actors of Shakespeare's time travelled to the low countries, to Scandinavia, and to Germany to perform, and during the following century companies from several countries roamed the continent. Such travel diminished markedly during the eighteenth century, however, so that the first small interchanges between London and Paris in the early 1800s were a totally new experience for both actors and audiences. Touring English actors in Paris in the 1820s created a sensation and contributed in no small measure to the development of the French romantic drama. In 1832 the director of Covent Garden, himself a Frenchman (the first foreign director in the history of that theatre), imported a series of foreign stars, culminating in leading actors from the Comédie Française itself. The Italian actress Carolina Internari attempted as early as 1830 to join this movement by taking a company to Paris, but their repertoire seemed to the French rather stuffy and old-fashioned and Internari was forced to give up this first modern attempt at Italian international touring.

The cross-channel visits of the 1820s and 1830s were followed by the more ambitious tours of the French actress Rachel, who may be considered the first international star. In 1841 she dazzled the London theatrical world, and returned there four times with continual unqualified success. She also toured

24

through Europe, gaining the applause of commoners and royalty alike. Then in 1855 she was astonishingly challenged and in the opinion of many eclipsed on her own ground in Paris by a new star from Italy, Adelaide Ristori.

Ristori's tour was not essentially different from the Internari project of 1830, but the conditions in Paris were now far more favorable. Where Internari had encountered a city in revolutionary upheaval, Ristori came to a city at peace and filled with pleasure-seeking crowds drawn to a major Exposition. During the twenty-five years since the Internari tour, the unsettled political conditions in Italy had led to the establishment of a large expatriate Italian community in Paris, which provided a basic, sympathetic audience for Ristori that Internari lacked. Finally, and ultimately most importantly, many of the leading authors and critics of Paris, headed by Jules Janin, were tired of what they felt to be artistic arrogance in Rachel and were eager to discover and support a rival to her.

All of this combined to win for Ristori a striking success in Paris, so great that it was widely (and no doubt falsely) believed that the shame of her crushing defeat drove Rachel to the unprecedented experiment of a tour to America. Whatever the French actress's motives, the American tour, exhausting and ill-organized, proved catastrophic for her. In weak health before the tour even began, she collapsed in Charleston, South Carolina, cancelled the remainder of the tour, and returned home, never to perform again. This left Ristori, at the age of 33, in undisputed possession of the title of Europe's leading actress, and she lost no time in solidifying this by embarking on tours to the countries already visited by Rachel, and then far beyond.

The Parisian triumph of 1855 attracted the attention of the director of the London Lyceum, already (due to the recent burning of Covent Garden) involved in the booking of Italian opera. He signed Ristori for a British engagement in 1856 with 15–18 performances in London and 3–6 in the provinces.[1] According to her memoirs, several English literary figures reproached her during this first London engagement for not including a Shakespearian play in her repertoire. Probably the possibility had not even occurred to her, since it was during this same season that Rossi and Salvini were demonstrating for the first time that Shakespeare could be successfully performed by Italian actors. Her reported excuse to her English friends, that Shakespeare's demands were too great in scenery and cast for a touring company, is not very convincing, since the historical pageants of Giacometti, always an important part of her repertoire, made much greater demands. In any case, she reports that her fears were alleviated by these friends' assurance that in England Shakespeare was regularly cut and arranged according to the needs and tastes of any given performance situation, and that audiences made no objection to this.[2]

Ristori's great roles were such tragic queens as Mary Stuart, Medea, and Phaedra, and it was not easy for her to find a similar vehicle in Shakespeare. She finally decided upon Lady Macbeth, suggesting to Carcano that he rework his translation to place more emphasis on this part, if possible adding a scene so that she might die on stage. Despite his admiration for Ristori, Carcano refused to commit such "sacrileges,"[3] and Ristori was forced to use the original Carcano text, though heavily edited to emphasize her role. This adaptation was the highlight of her second British tour, in 1857, and her interpretation, especially of the sleepwalking scene, was lavishly praised.

When she returned to London the following summer, *Macbeth* was her opening production, but the audience was disappointingly small and the play was not repeated. Indeed, attendance for all of her offerings in London was small; apparently in three successive summers Ristori had come close to exhausting the interest of the English public in her work. During the next several years, therefore, she toured elsewhere in Europe, to Scandinavia, Russia, Greece, Holland, Germany, Spain, and Portugal. Inevitably she was drawn eventually to attempt what had proven beyond the capability of her predecessor Rachel, a tour to the new world.

In 1861 Ristori signed a contract with the American impresario Bernard Ullman, but the coming of the Civil War thwarted these plans,[4] and it was not until the war was over that another entrepreneur, Jacob Grau, would succeed in introducing Ristori to America. Much had changed in America during the eleven years between the visit of Rachel and that of Ristori. In the aftermath of the war, that period of major industrial and economic expansion which Mark Twain characterized as the Gilded Age had begun, and a new pleasure- and culture-seeking public was now eager to welcome Europe's great international stars into its midst. Nor was the public the only thing that had changed during these years. Improved transportation and communication made the arrangement of extensive tours more manageable even if not yet really comfortable, and the business of theatre marketing and publicity was rapidly gaining in power and effectiveness. The sort of press agentry that reached its zenith with such touring stars as Bernhardt really began with Ristori. Rachel's father and brother, who arranged her American tour, had little idea of how to increase their profits beyond raising prices, performing in large halls, and ruthlessly exploiting the unhappy Rachel. The power of publicity was virtually unknown to them.

With Jacob Grau it was a different matter. He had begun his theatre career selling librettos for Max Maretzck, then graduated to speculating in tickets for Bernard Ullman and Maurice Strakosch at the Academy of Music, and had learned much from the struggles of these pioneers to establish and maintain Italian opera in New York with largely imported and unknown singers. They learned from such masters as P. T. Barnum the power of publicity to draw audiences and applied these lessons with increasing bravura and success. Thus Strakosch attracted substantial crowds in 1857 to hear the tenor Tiberini by billing him as the linear descendent of the Roman Emperor Tiberius, and in 1858 touted his prima donna Marietta Piccolomini as the granddaughter of Schiller's hero and a direct descendant of Charlemagne.

Grau became director of the Academy in 1862, but his entrepreneurial skills proved no match for the problems of the war years. In 1866 he made a new beginning by taking over the Théâtre Français (opened the previous year as an outlet for French plays in New York) and announcing a season dominated by the first American appearance of Ristori. The venture was more risky than might at first appear. A certain audience had been developed for imported operatic stars, but leading actors performing in languages other than English in the spoken theatre was another matter, and the single precedent of Rachel was not encouraging. Most critics frankly predicted financial disaster for Grau, especially after it was announced that he had risked an unprecedented $50,000 in advance payment for the tour.

Such announcements, however, were themselves part of a massive and well-orchestrated publicity campaign as unprecedented as Grau's investment. For months before Ristori's arrival the leading American newspapers were provided with information on the coming star, stressing those concerns which Grau felt would most intrigue the nouveaux riches of the 1860s—the sumptuousness of Ristori's wardrobe, the expense of bringing her entire company, the fact that she had not only performed before, but been received by and honored by European royalty, and her own marriage to a marquis in an aristocratic but also highly romantic love match. Finally, of course, Ristori was presented as a kind of artistic world champion, the successful rival of the departed Rachel. All such publicity attempted, with great success, to convince the American public that they were about to witness an artistic, cultural, and social event of the first magnitude, an event which would inevitably be attended by everyone with any social or cultural pretensions whatever.

Even the public with little interest in such matters would have found it hard to escape contact with Grau's publicity. Every step of Ristori's journey to America was announced in the major New York papers. The *Times, Herald,* and *Sunday Mercury* all ran stories on her September 1 departure from Brest. Her arrival in New York was front-page news and during the several weeks before her first performance not a day passed without fresh news stories. Grau housed his star at the fashionable Fifth Avenue Hotel, and arranged for her to be constantly in activity, receiving distinguished visitors and delegations at her hotel, or attending major social events and openings of expositions. The *Herald* and other papers dutifully followed all this activity with regular features bearing such headings as "Her doings today," "Movements of Madame Ristori" and "Her Third Day in New York." Advance copies of the *Macbeth* libretto were sent to social organizations and local publicity outlets and a whole series of products were launched, the publicity for which added to the growing clamor: "Ristori Eau-de-Cologne," "Ristori candies," "Ristori mascara." Nor was the production itself forgotten. As the Théâtre Français was prepared for the opening, other news stories appeared about the elaborateness and expense of the scenery and costumes to be displayed there.[5]

The success of this enormous campaign was apparent as soon as the public sale of tickets began. The box office was scheduled to open at 9:00 A.M., but lines began to form by 4:00 P.M. the previous day, and some 2,000 prospective patrons and 500 messenger boys representing others were waiting when the tickets went on sale. Police were needed to control the crowds, and the first week was already sold out by noon. Among the first purchasers were a considerable number of speculators and, although Grau had charged the highest prices ever seen in New York—one to four dollars per seat—tickets were soon changing hands for as much as $50. Such scandalous speculation was roundly condemned in the newspapers, which of course only added to the frenzy.

Long before the New York engagement was completed, it was clear that Grau was going to win handsomely on his $50,000 investment. The engagement lasted five weeks, during which time Ristori performed twenty times in Manhattan and five times at the Brooklyn Academy of Music. Receipts averaged around $3,000 per night and on several occasions ran over $4,000. The largest amount ever recorded in a single evening in a European theatre had been gained by Ristori at a benefit in Moscow. This was $3,600, a record broken many times during her American tour. This success, of course, made it certain that Grau's experiment would be repeated in coming years by himself and by other entrepreneurs, one of whom, his nephew Maurice, was now beginning his career as Grau had begun his, selling librettos for the Ristori productions.

Ristori offered six plays during this first visit to New York, the most popular being *Medea*, *Mary Stuart*, and Giacometti's *Elizabeth*. *Macbeth* was the last presented, given only twice in New York and once in Brooklyn. It was well received, though distinctly less popular than Ristori's historical pageants. After two weeks in Boston, where she gave *Macbeth* once, the actress returned to New York to offer several additional plays, none of which proved as popular as her first selection. This pattern was repeated throughout the tour and Ristori's bookings soon came to reflect it. For one- or two-night engagements she would present either *Mary Stuart* (occasionally with the sleepwalking scene from *Macbeth* as an afterpiece) or *Elizabeth.* In the larger cities, such as Philadelphia, Baltimore, Cincinnati, or Memphis, where she remained a week or two, she might give these plays twice, along with single performances of *Medea, Phaedra,* or *Macbeth.*

The tour began by covering the major cities of the Eastern seaboard, essentially the same ground covered by Rachel a decade before. Then Ristori struck out into new territory, the American West. Major cities were now easily if not especially comfortably accessible by railroad, and early in January the company headed for Chicago by way of Detroit and Cincinnati. From Chicago they turned south to St. Louis and Memphis, to arrive in New Orleans early in February, where they remained through the carnival season.

Everywhere Ristori was anticipated by an unprecedented publicity campaign and everywhere she received the same rapturous welcome she had enjoyed in New York. Other entrepreneurs sought to capitalize on the Ristori craze, so that a whole series of Ristori endorsements helped to swell the tide of publicity. On the front page of the *Chicago Tribune* of 23 January 1867, the day of Ristori's arrival in that city, appeared a lengthy advertisement with the bold heading RISTORI by the manufacturers of Dr. Chaussier's "Empress for the Hair." This quoted in full a letter of thanks from the actress, who had been given a bottle of this preparation in New York. The notice concluded: "If any other testimony than that of the fashionable world, who universally use this incomparable preparation to the exclusion of all others, were necessary, it would be found in this most strong and positive endorsement of this preparation from the Italian Queen of Song." The expression "Queen of Song," repeated several times in the advertisement, indicates clearly enough that by this time Ristori's name was famous enough to attract attention on its own, even among those who did not even know what she was actually doing.

The publicity campaign snowballed as quotations from enthusiastic reviews in New York, Boston, Philadelphia and then in the cities of the West (Chicago papers called the visit "the greatest dramatic triumph on record") could be added to the enticements promised the patrons in cities where she was yet to appear. Then, for those potential spectators who might be overwhelmed by this artistic brilliance and by the actress's connections with European aristocracy, there were releases stressing the domestic side of her character, as may be seen in a front page story appearing February 12 in the *New Orleans Times-Picayune*. After praising Ristori's "wonderful industry" as the true source of her greatness, the article continued:

> She carries her own cook with her, and superintends the preparation of all her meals. She arranges the economy of her own household, like any other good house wife. She watches, like a mother, over her son and daughter, and like a good wife, loves her husband. She personally attends to the wants of her servants, and sees they are well fed and housed. When she travels abroad, she packs her own trunks. She likes, above all things, to have her own house. If she resides long in any city, she always does have it. She has one in New York and is looking out for one in New Orleans. She is fond of domestic life, its quietude, its honesty, its purity, and though very fond of society, desires to be the mistress of her own household. Thus, true and honest and natural in all the relations of life, fond and capable of studying tragedy at its fountain sources, she has become the queen of tragedy, not by any wonderful transformation, but by the simple laws of nature.

From New Orleans Ristori went on to Mobile, then returned to Chicago by way of Nashville and Louisville. She then followed the cities of the lake shores to Buffalo and continued across upstate New York to Boston and finally back to New York City. Her tour concluded with a series of benefit performances, one of which was *Macbeth* on May 16 for the Ladies'

Southern Relief Association. Following her departure two days later, the *New York Times* of May 19 offered some statistics on her remarkable tour. She had given 370 performances in 30 cities during her eight months in America, travelling 18,000 miles in all. Her total receipts were an astonishing $430,000.

After such a success, Grau not surprisingly made arrangements for Ristori to return the following season before she left America. Her 1867–68 tour was even longer and more successful than the first, though she covered less territory, concentrating on the cities of the Northeast with a two-month interval in Havana. Her repertoire was reduced also to her most popular proven favorites, headed by *Elizabeth,* with one major new production, Giacometti's *Marie Antoinette. Macbeth* was dropped entirely from this tour, though on a single occasion in Philadelphia, *Medea* was followed by what was billed as the last act of *Macbeth*—probably only the sleepwalking scene.

After tours through South American cities and Eastern Europe, Ristori returned to London for the fourth time in the summer of 1873, playing a month at Drury Lane and returning in the fall for another month at the Opéra Comique. Perhaps the most outstanding feature of this tour was her first performance of the sleepwalking scene from *Macbeth* in English, though this was not the central new offering of the tour as the actress suggests in her memoirs.[6] She brought to London two major new productions, *Renée de France* and *Lucrezia Borgia,* which were clearly selected to stimulate fresh interest in the public. With the *Macbeth* scene she was taking a much greater risk, and it in any case could be used only as a sort of encore, not as the feature of an evening. She did not at first even attempt it in English, but offered it in Italian, as she had done before, as part of her benefit at the close of her July performances at Drury Lane. When she returned to London in October she set to work preparing the scene in English for the benefit which would close that engagement.

Ristori had studied English as a girl, but this was virtually a new beginning for her. She was warmly encouraged by friends in London, especially by Mrs. Lucy Ward and her daughter Geneviève, who had a particular interest in *Macbeth.* Geneviève had gained an international reputation as an operatic singer during the same years when Ristori's fame was established, but her voice had been permanently damaged by an attack of diphtheria while she was on tour in Cuba. Now in 1873 Geneviève was planning to launch herself in a new career as a dramatic actress and was preparing Lady Macbeth as her premier role. Ristori studied with the Wards, apparently to their mutual benefit, for Ristori's command of English and Ward's general interpretation were both warmly praised. Ward, however, had to succeed in the provinces before coming to London, and, arriving later on the scene, was often called by critics Ristori's pupil. Ristori acknowledged a much closer tie, calling her *La mia Doppia* (my double).

Every precaution was exercised concerning Ristori's English-language debut. Years later in her memoirs Geneviève Ward described the assiduous efforts of her "illustrious pupil": "She took a sheet of foolscap, copied the text, then wrote it out in Italian, as she heard me pronounce it, with the Italian orthography. Above this she would have another line, with marks up and down like crescents, and all sorts of other notes to aid her in getting the right accent."[7] After working on the sleepwalking scene for a fortnight with the Wards, Ristori invited London's leading dramatic critics to her dwelling for a private preview, informing them that if their judgments were unfavorable she would abandon the project. She reports that they corrected only two words and urged her to continue. Accordingly she offered the scene in English at the close of each of her last two London performances, to enormous applause. With such strong encouragement, she began a study of the entire play in English, but after a few months gave this up as beyond her power.

In 1874 Ristori undertook a tour around the world, beginning in South America and arriving in New York in February of 1875. Her former manager, Jacob Grau, was dead, but his business had been inherited by his nephew Maurice, who gladly undertook the arrangements for a new series of Ristori appearances. She crossed the United States and departed for Australia from San Francisco in June. The English-language sleepwalking scene was now in her regular repertoire and was presented at least once in every major city she visited. For her final benefit in

San Francisco on June 18 she gave a remarkable display of versatility, offering acts 1, 3, and 5 of *Mary Stuart* and act 4 of *Elizabeth* in Italian, the sleepwalking scene in English, Lamartine's poem *L'Isolement* in French, and Joan of Arc's farewell speech in Spanish. She was received on this tour with honor but without the passionate enthusiasm which had greeted her in the past, everywhere acknowledged as one of the world's great actresses, but also as an artist rather past her prime whose interpretations had become familiar and were even beginning to seem a bit old-fashioned.

After her world tour Ristori continued to perform for another five years, then, at the age of fifty-eight, retired to Rome. In her leisure hours she returned to the long-abandoned project of learning *Macbeth* in English, and became now so fascinated by it that she resolved to return again with this production to London and America. During the month of July, 1882, she appeared at Drury Lane, giving *Macbeth* for two weeks and *Elizabeth* for two, both in English. She then toured through the English provinces, meeting with great success still. Her memoirs claim that she returned to London with these plays the following year, but the records seem to indicate that she appeared on this tour only in the provinces.[8]

Maurice Grau made the arrangements for her final American tour in 1884–85. This last tour was also her longest and most extensive, ranging from coast to coast and lasting seven months—a major feat for an actress in her sixty-third year. Thanks to a contract which gave her forty percent of her gross receipts, the most ever given to an artist on tour, these final American appearances were the most profitable of her career, but the audiences remained much as they had been in 1875— moderate and respectful, but not enthusiastic. The *New York Herald* of 15 March 1884 reported that she was received with "noble-hearted sympathy" as befitted "a fabled relic of a storied past." The English-language productions, with which she surely hoped to arouse some of the old public enthusiasm, were regarded more as curiosities than as new evidence of her artistic power. The *Chicago Tribune* of November 23 noted that she spoke distinctly in calmer moments but that her English "fell like tangled underbrush in her path when she rose to higher endeavor." Apparently she had less trace of a specific accent than other foreign stars who attempted English roles, so that individual words were clear enough, though with whole phrases the rhythm was sufficiently alien to disturb both poetry and meaning. Not a few reviewers, while complimenting her on her accomplishment, suggested that, all things considered, her Lady Macbeth had been more effective in Italian.

Ristori's usual pattern during this tour was to present *Elizabeth* twice a week and *Macbeth* once, occasionally adding the sleepwalking scene as an afterpiece to one of the Italian plays still in her repertoire. Just before the end of the tour she appeared twice in *Macbeth* with Edwin Booth, once in Brooklyn and once in Philadelphia. Her final performance in America was yet another linguistic experiment—a production of *Mary Stuart* at New York's Thalia Theatre with Ristori speaking English and the rest of the company German.

Following this tour Ristori began her true retirement, though she occasionally gave recitations for special events in Rome and appeared a final time in *Macbeth* with Ernesto Rossi at Rome's Teatro Apollo in 1887. She died in Rome in 1906.

3
Ristori's *Macbeth*

The version of *Macbeth* offered by Ristori was the farthest removed from the original of any of the Italian Shakespearian texts, in fact an adaptation of Carcano's translation. Ristori and her English Adapter, "Mr. Clark" (possibly Charles Crowden Clarke, a contemporary editor of Shakespeare's works), respected Carcano's wish to add no new material to the play, but their extensive cuttings transformed it radically. In Italy, where audiences were accustomed to theatrical performances lasting for hours, with ballets or musical numbers between the acts and a farce afterpiece, the presentation of one of Carcano's translations essentially uncut presented no problems in timing, but, when the Italian stars began to tour to England and America, they encountered a much more inflexible theatrical culture. Performances were expected to begin at eight and to end by ten-thirty or eleven at the very latest, requiring significant cutting in all of these Shakespearian works.[1]

Understandably Ristori, Salvini, and Rossi all cut the plays in such a way as to emphasize their own roles; any other choice would have run quite counter to the dynamic of these tours. At the same time, this process clearly created a greater distortion of the original text in the case of Lady Macbeth than in those of Hamlet, Othello, or Lear. The reviews, significantly, frequently refer to Ristori's play as *Lady Macbeth* even though the original title (according to Carcano's wishes) always appeared in programs and advertisements. The *London Atlas* of 11 July 1857 complained that "everything has been sacrificed for the part of Lady Macbeth. We protest against the heresy." General critical reaction, however, was more in line with that of the *London Observer* of July 6, which observed that: "Much less liberty . . . has been taken with Shakespeare in adapting *Macbeth* to the peculiar resources of the Italian company than in many so-called revivals of the poet." In either case, critics agreed in hailing Ristori as the greatest Lady Macbeth of her generation.

The first two scenes of the original play were cut entirely, so that Ristori's version began with Macbeth's encounter with the witches. This was, in fact, the only appearance of the witches in the play. The fourth scene was also cut, so that the entrance of Lady Macbeth reading her husband's letter directly followed the scene between Macbeth, Banquo, and the witches. Ristori wished to indicate in her reading that the witches inspired the same awe in her through this narration as they would have done had she actually encountered them, so she attempted to live the emotions of the preceding scene as she read. Such lines as "they made themselves air, into which they vanished" were delivered with an intonation of deep awe and followed by a contemplative silence. The letter read, she made an even longer pause, gloomy and fearful, weighing her visions against her misgivings. Then, her decision made, she began with grim determination the line

> Glamis thou art and Cawdor, and shalt be
> What thou art promised . . .

laying almost supernatural stress on the "shalt be," an inflection which recalled to many the memorable reading of the last great Lady Macbeth, Mrs. Siddons.

Her following lines concerning Macbeth's nature she gave as if they were directly addressed to him as he stood before her. The awesome invocation to the spirits of evil following the arrival of Duncan's messenger allowed Ristori to give full rein to the satanic side of her Lady Macbeth. She began it in a cavernous voice, then modulated almost to the hiss of a serpent, and then began a tremendous crescendo, compared by one critic to the swelling of an organ, as her figure seemed to expand and her eyes light up with infernal fire. This passion, at its peak, was turned into an exaggerated cry of joy as Macbeth entered. Ristori now abruptly changed to a tone of coldness and reserve, as if to indicate her ability to control herself as well as her husband. Here was the first clear signal of that dominance which was one of the most striking features of her interpretation. One critic called Macbeth "the veriest slave of her will and pleasure. In the murder scene she was everything, he was nothing—in fact, all throughout she overshadowed and extinguished the wretched creature."[2] Not infrequently reviewers considered this domination excessive; the *New York Times* viewed Ristori's Lady Macbeth as "gaunt, unfeminine, harsh and even overbearing," and the *Tribune* called her "a bloody-minded virago."

This impression was no doubt due in part to the series of weak actors, both Italian and English, which, according to the tradition of the star system, were selected to support Ristori, but the actress's own vision of this character clearly contributed to the effect. In her memoirs she describes Lady Macbeth as a "monster in human likeness" with "inhuman power" over her husband. "She becomes the Satanic spirit of the body of Macbeth. He has a hard struggle between the 'wishing and not wishing;' that woman, that serpent, becomes absolute mistress of this man, entwines him in her grasp, and no human power can ever tear him from it."[3] The force of her evil was thus much more direct and brutal than English or American audiences were accustomed to, and this frequently led to negative comments on her lack of subtlety, both in actions (after reading Macbeth's letter she threw it out the door) and in lines ("And when goes hence" was a blunt invitation to murder, with no attempt to disguise that implication). Macbeth's "We will speak further" was delivered as a weak attempt to resist his wife's driving force, an attempt which she overwhelmed both physically and vocally. Inducing him to pass his left arm around her waist, she then placed his right index finger on her lips to force his silence, and then pushed him gently but firmly backward offstage into the wings, delivering the line "Leave all the rest to me" with a sort of heroic disdain. She was, reported Henry

Morley, "smiling the while with firm-set lips and nodding satisfaction at her work. He is in her power; he moves at her urging."[4]

The blunt, cruel tone of this first scene changed to one of perfidious simulated sweetness and humility when Lady Macbeth welcomed Duncan to the castle. Ristori was praised for the subtlety of this scene, letting a false tone slip into her voice, a false expression play faintly across her face, enough to make her duplicity clear to the audience without suggesting that Duncan might observe anything suspicious in her greeting. A few reviewers felt that this rapid change of manner and this carefully managed hypocrisy was somewhat too Italianate for Shakespeare, however, and drew uneasy comparisons with Lucrezia Borgia or the Medici.

For the following scene, as Macbeth was pressed to the murder, Ristori returned to her vigorous and direct attack, with even more vehemence than in her opening scene. Particularly effective was her reading of the passage:

> I have given suck; and know
> How tender 'tis to love the babe that milks me:
> I would, while it was smiling in my face,
> Have plucked my nipple from his boneless gums
> And dashed the brains out, had I so sworn as you
> Have done to this.

Ristori went through the described situation precisely as if she were actively engaged in it—holding the babe to her breast, tearing it passionately from her, hurling it to the ground, watching its last agonies, and then drawing herself up, proud and resolute, over this imagined horror. The *Saturday Review* cited this passage as a central example of Ristori's style:

> This rapid succession of distinct points of acting, this resolution of a general idea into the energetic exhibition of its parts, is the leading peculiarity of Madame Ristori's performances. It is successful with her simply because it is natural. She belongs to a nation accustomed to express every play of passion and every shade of feeling by gesticulation. She of course has subordinated the national habit to the require-

ments and possibilities of art, and every word and movement has been evidently most carefully studied; but still this
sense of pantomimic gestures is fundamentally Italian, and is
neither to be criticised as excessive or unnatural in Madame
Ristori, nor to be raised into an indispensable part of high
acting. It is simply something which we admire and enjoy in
this particular actress.[5]

Such point-by-point illustration of key passages seems indeed
to have been a characteristic of Italian acting at least of this
generation, for the performances of both Salvini and Rossi contained passages of much the same type, and were doubtless
quite helpful to audiences who did not understand Italian.
Macbeth's agreement, "I am settled," caused Ristori's face to
lighten with exultation, but she emphasized her continuing
control over her husband by half accompanying, half leading
him from the stage as she had done in their first scene together.
The second act was played with almost nothing cut except
the drunken porter scene and was thus more faithful to the
original than any contemporary English acting version. Lady
Macbeth continued to appear as the visible, driving force behind her husband's actions. She hovered in the background
during the "Is this a dagger" soliloquy, stepping forward at the
end to half lead, half push Macbeth over Duncan's threshold.
The actual murder scene was quietly and solemnly rendered
(thus, some noted, missing the sense of horror which Charlotte
Cushman, for example, created in it). Even when Ristori
showed her hands red with the blood of the grooms, her tone
of defiance was powerful, but hushed; whatever terror she felt
appeared to come not from the deed just committed but from
the possibility that her vacillating and fearful mate would be
unable to stay the course. Ristori herself observed that the
fright Lady Macbeth experiences when she hears the unexpected knocking at the gate comes not from apprehension that
the crime will soon be discovered but from concern that Macbeth in his state of prostration will betray everything.[6]
This was the key also to her much-praised pantomiming of
the ensuing scene, when the murder of the King is discovered.
Ristori brilliantly contrasted her affected horror at the murder

with her real anxiety for what her husband would say. Observed the *Saturday Review:* "Her simulated shrinking, and shuddering at the thought of blood—apparently so true to nature, and yet its insincerity displayed by a single lightning gleam of suspicion and doubt whether her irresolute husband might betray himself—all this, without a single word spoken to convey its significance, elevates acting into something akin to a function of the plastic art."[7] There was some difference of opinion among critics concerning Ristori's faint. Not surprisingly, those who were most struck by the cold-blooded calculation of her Lady Macbeth were convinced that her collapse was mere deception, designed to draw attention from her unstable spouse. No one suggests any specific action performed by Ristori which would clearly indicate this, however, and her playing of such scenes as the discovery of the murder or the banquet provides strong evidence that when she wished to show deception she could do so both subtly and unmistakably. The majority of critics, who accepted her faint as an honest reaction, would thus seem to have the stronger case. Ristori appears to have prepared somewhat for the faint by relaxing her tension a bit after Macbeth reveals that he has killed the grooms and thus become master of the situation. With his firmness assured, her natural reactions can at last be permitted play. Morley suggests that Macbeth's lines concerning the murdered Duncan were given a special force by Ristori fainting at this point:

> She is struck with real horror as Macbeth tells how he had found the murdered king, "His silver skin laced with his golden blood." She had before passed rapidly over the admission to herself that she with her own hand would have killed Duncan "had he not resembled her father as he slept." She had hurried over the thought as one not to be dwelt upon, and showed a fine taste in so doing. Macbeth afterwards inadvertently thrusts it home into her heart, and then the point is made that ninety-nine actresses in a hundred would assuredly have tried to make before.[8]

The first scene of act 3 was cut by Ristori, so that the act opened with the Macbeth-Lady Macbeth dialogue after the dispatching of Banquo's murderers. Here the actress gave her first clear indication of the inner torment which was to find its eventual full expression in the sleepwalking scene. The *Athenæum* called her look and gesture in response to Macbeth's line

> Duncan is in his grave,
> After life's fitful fever he sleeps well

an excellent proof that Ristori was a great actress "by right of forethought as well as impulse."

> The haggard weariness of her shrinking away from him to whom she had been listening,—making so clear and fearful a comment on the deed which "had murdered sleep"—and on the secret which, when slumber was at last won, the ghostlike tongue of slumber was to reveal . . . was poetry—dread, deep, and tragical—if there *be* poetry in acting.[9]

The scene of Banquo's murder being omitted, this interchange was followed directly by the banquet scene, one of the high points of the production. The *New York Times* of 3 January 1885 remarked that "the byplay of this scene is altogether admirable, and without resorting to any stage trickery the woman is made the central figure in the picture." This was achieved, of course, by focusing the scene upon Lady Macbeth's efforts to maintain the stability of the situation despite Macbeth's increasingly erratic behavior. Even as early as the arrival of the murderer, Lady Macbeth shared the focus of the murderer's dialogue with Macbeth by being the only person in the hall to observe this interchange. Thus she could play a dramatic double part, indulging in light conversation and sharing the toasts of the guests seated on their stools while at the same time casting fearful and questioning glances toward Macbeth at the door to warn him of the danger he was running. This tension mounted until it at last burst forth in the forced joviality of

> My royal lord,
> You do not give the cheer.

In her asides to Macbeth, Ristori employed gestures and a tone of voice strongly reminiscent of those she had used when incit-

ing him to murder, but with increasing desperation now. As if
to fortify her own courage she took a large cup of wine as
Macbeth was saying

> The times have been
> That, when the brains were out, the man would die,

and did not lay it down until after the next appearance of the
ghost. Finally the strain became too much for her. The forced
gaiety disappeared and she hushed the guests' questions and
hurried them away with an agitation almost as great as that of
Macbeth himself.

Left alone with Macbeth, Ristori abruptly shifted her mood
to what she called a counterscene of distress and failing power
as her Lady Macbeth realized at last the hopelessness of the
struggle. The color left her face, her voice became less determined, her movements were slow and faltering. In counterpoint to this, Macbeth at the beginning of the scene paced
wildly up and down until suddenly he encountered her directly and, becoming suddenly aware of her pallid features and
lack of movement, recoiled from her as if from another phantom. To his questions she replied with a weary, distant voice,
clearly prefiguring the agony to be revealed in the coming
sleepwalking scene. Still, the new mood was not entirely one of
withdrawal. Mixed with the weariness and sense of defeat was
a note of pity for Macbeth, the victim of her lust for power. In
her memoirs, Ristori described the gentle manner in which she
led him from the stage after her line "You lack the season of all
natures, sleep:"

> I take hold of his left hand with my right and place it over my
> right shoulder, then painfully bending my head in deep
> reflection and turning toward my husband with a look filled
> with remorse which is agitating my mind, I drag him toward
> our chamber in the same manner that one leads an insane
> person. When reaching the limit of the stage Macbeth, fright-
> ened by the tail of his cloak trailing at my feet, again shud-
> ders suddenly. Then, with a quick turn, I pass on the other
> side of him, and try to master the terror with which I am also
> seized in spite of myself. Using a little violence, I succeed in

pushing him behind the wings, while quieting him with af-
fectionate gestures.[10]

At this point the third act ended, the final two scenes—the
first with Hecate and the witches, the other between the two
Scots lords—both being cut. The witches' prophecy scene
opening the next act was also cut, as was the murder of Lady
Macduff and her children, so that Ristori's final act (acts 4 and 5
were combined) began with the dialogue between Malcolm and
Macduff. The sleepwalking scene which followed was the pin-
nacle of Ristori's interpretation, the most lavishly praised scene
and the scene which she often presented as a set piece of its
own, first in Italian, and later in English.

The critic Laura Caretti has observed a striking similarity in
all of Ristori's major characters, calling her repertoire "an or-
ganic series of moralities, where the bourgeois dichotomies of
appearance and reality, the normal and the deviant, the tragic
struggle between Jekyll and Hyde is developed as in a Dickens
novel."[11] In each of these dramas a moral struggle was depicted
between passion and conscience in the central character, and in
each passion was shown as ruling the character in the early
actions of the play, only to be gradually overcome by conscience, with the ultimate result of the sacrificial death of the
sinful body before the fall of the curtain. To make Lady Macbeth fit into this pattern Ristori had not only to reduce Macbeth
to essentially a pawn of his ambitious spouse, but also to remove most of the suggestions of supernatural forces at work or
even of external political considerations. The central conflict of
her *Macbeth* was in the soul of her character.

Under these circumstances, the sleepwalking scene became
the inevitable focal point of the production. The banquet scene
served as a bridge between the early and late parts of the play,
moving from triumphant if precarious security to anxiety and
fear, but it was in the sleepwalking scene that Ristori was able
to portray to the full the suffering penitent who served as the
moral counterweight to the ambitious demon of the opening
acts. This scene was so often presented and so highly admired
that her interpretation of it can be reconstructed almost line by
line. It was a chilling scene, arousing in its audiences a mixture
of wonder at the art of the actress and awe and dread at her

harrowing creation. The spectral quality suggested in her previous scene now became dominant, and her fixed, sightless gaze, her slow movements, her mysterious whisper gave the audience an impression more of death than of sleep. Her costume, suggesting the tormented penitent, added to this impression—pallid makeup, a long white robe, a white coif wound around her head, the only relief from this pallor being her blue-black hair escaping loosely from its confines. All political references were removed from the doctor's lines, as well indeed as all of his scientific observations and his plan to "set down what comes from here." He becomes merely a choral voice of horror and pity, a guide to the reactions of the spectators.

Ristori entered the stage with eyes fixed, like an automaton, dragging her feet as if they were weighted. Her breathing was difficult and labored. Mechanically placing the lamp on the table, she advanced to the footlights, pretending to see the drops of blood on her hands, rubbing them and taking into them imaginary water to wash them, a gesture which she repeated several times during the scene. All her movements were slow, "intercepted," Ristori says, "by my chilled nerves." At the footlights she began to speak in a low, murmuring tone, almost a whisper, but perfectly audible: "Yet here's a spot."

After listening a moment, she said softly: "One: two: why then 'tis time to do't," then, as if answering: "Hell is murky." Her lines about the old man's blood and the Thane of Fife were delivered as delirious cries, followed by a moment of silent regard of her hands and then the line: "What, will these hands ne'er be clean," delivered in a tone between rage and sadness. After a convulsive rubbing motion, she seemed to see her husband before her, and whispered excitedly in his ear: "No more o' that, my lord." As the doctor and gentlewoman spoke, she smelled her hands, preparing for the line: "Here's the smell of the blood still." The "Oh, oh, oh!" ending this line she spoke as if an internal shudder had stopped her breath; then she remained with her head thrown back, breathing slowly in a deep lethargy.

As the doctor and the gentlewoman spoke again Ristori returned in pantomime to the scene of the murder, feverishly reenacting that event like a character from Dante's *Inferno*, forced to recount her guilt while suffering at the same time the full weight of conscience and remorse. Bending her body, she advanced slowly and mysteriously toward the right side of the stage, where Duncan's chamber was located. She pretended to hear her husband's quick step and inclined her ear to listen to his report. Then in an outburst of agitation and joy she began the line "wash your hands, put on your nightgown." A great emotion and the first touch of fear came with the lines "to bed, to bed! There's knocking at the gate." She took her imaginary husband by both hands and seemed to drag him with great effort from the stage, speaking "to bed, to bed, to bed" in a half-suffocated voice. The tradition of the English stage called for Lady Macbeth to pick up her candle and retire upstage center through the door by which she had entered. Ristori created a final unexpected and striking effect by leaving the candle and making her painful exit off through the wings, as if going at once to oblivion. A typical reaction to the scene was reported by the *Illustrated London News* of 8 July 1882:

> Her acting was really and admirably great. She hushed her audience to death-like silence; every one of her gestures was anxiously watched by the large and appreciative audience present; and when she uttered her final "to bed!" and flitted rather than walked from the stage, such a storm of plaudits arose, enforcing again and again her recall, as has rarely been heard within the time-honoured walls of old Drury.

After this great scene, the climax of Ristori's production, short work was made of the rest of the play. Dunsinane castle was attacked and Macbeth dispatched within a few minutes of dialogue, in a single page of the libretto. This gave Macbeth little time to reflect upon his fate, but, considering the inadequacy of the supporting actor usually playing this role and the impression created by the rest of the play that Macbeth was really simply a pawn in the hands of his powerful wife, no one complained about this. Indeed most reviewers seemed relieved to be rid of him as quickly as possible. A nod was made to complete the form of the play, but audiences had come not to see Shakespeare, but to see Ristori, and, whatever the text might suggest, when she left the stage, for them the play was over.

4

The Tours of Tommaso Salvini

The success of Ristori's international tours, coupled with the generally unsettled and discouraging state of the Italian theatre in the years immediately following political unification, encouraged other leading actors to seek their fortunes outside their homeland. The most famous of these, rivaling even Ristori herself, was Tommaso Salvini. He began, as we have seen, as a student of the great Gustavo Modena and achieved his first great success in 1848 at the age of nineteen as Alfieri's Oreste (the young Ristori played Elettra in the same production). He was already generally recognized as one of Italy's leading players when he scored his double triumph with Othello and Hamlet in 1856. The welcome which Ristori received in Paris encouraged Salvini to follow her example, and in 1857 he appeared at the Salle Ventadour, which had hosted Ristori the previous two seasons. His reception was at first indifferent, possibly because, unlike Ristori, he had the temerity to open with one of the French classics, Voltaire's *Zaïre*, given, of course, in Italian. Salvini's countrymen considered this work one of his greatest, but the French critics were not impressed. Alfieri's *Saul* fared even worse, but then came *Othello*, an unexpected success which more than redeemed the near-failure of the previous offerings. English and American tourists in Paris came too, and one of the latter, a woman who, according to Salvini, wielded "much influence among the publishing enterprises of North America," urged him to consider an American tour. Salvini was not tempted. The Paris venture had come too close to failure for him to commit himself at this time to an even more problematic undertaking. He returned to Italy and did no more foreign touring for more than a decade.

Still his reputation continued to grow, and not merely within the boundaries of Italy. The peninsula was a standard cultural attraction for English tourists and these began to send home glowing reports of Italy's best-known actor. The Brownings saw his *Othello* and *Hamlet* in Florence in June of 1859 and considered them outstanding. Browning later called Salvini's *Oedipus* "absolutely the finest effort of art" he had ever beheld—"not only the finest in the art of acting, but in any art whatsoever."[1] The progress of Salvini's career could be traced in the occasional notes submitted to London journals from their Italian correspondents, and the 30 January 1864 issue of the *Athenæum* contained a letter from Mary C. Clarke in Genoa with a detailed description of Salvini's *Othello*. She concluded that Salvini's "dramatic genius" created productions "so true to universal human nature that, even through the disadvantage of a translated version, they go straight to the hearts of men."[2] In May of 1870 Charlotte Cushman saw *Othello* in Rome and without qualification pronounced it "the greatest the world has ever seen."[3]

By the end of the 1860s, when Salvini, increasingly discouraged by theatrical conditions at home, was ready again to consider the alternative of international traveling, he found a public ready to receive him with the greatest enthusiasm. He began modestly, with a trip to Spain and Portugal; then in 1871 he toured South America, with sufficient success to launch him on a career of regular touring. The South American trip was followed almost at once by an invitation from Maurice Grau to tour the United States in 1873–74. When Grau inherited his uncle's booking agency he began working on a fairly regular basis with Charles Chizzola, an Italian manager-impresario located in Paris. Chizzola served as liaison between first Jacob, then Maurice, Grau and Salvini and accompanied Salvini and his company to America on this first tour.

Maurice followed his uncle's example in launching an impressive publicity campaign for the new star, as Celso Salvini reports in his biography of the actor:

> Everywhere there were photographic pictures; lithographs by the thousands, in a hundred different poses, distributed to every part of the city; his name in block capitals on every wall, in every public place, on the public coaches, on the trams, on the sidewalks; with small leaflets and pictures in every restaurant and bar, even on the trays that were carried to the tables. But what surpassed everything else were the pamphlets and biographies: thousands of biographies everywhere, in the hotels, in the theatres, in all public places, scattered along the thoroughfares by huge coaches— biographies each one different from the next, containing the most arbitrary and fantastic things, and truthful in nothing except Salvini's name.[4]

Once again this overwhelming publicity campaign proved successful in whipping up public interest and enthusiasm. Tickets for the performances were in great demand and when Salvini opened with *Othello* in New York the house was full to overflowing. Critics and general public alike were dazzled by his unconventional but powerful interpretation. For most theatregoers of this generation it became the definitive *Othello*. Naturally Salvini dominated the occasion, but the company which he had brought with him, including many actors with whom he had long been associated in Italy, was also widely praised. Signora Paimonti played Desdemona and Salvini's younger brother Alessandro was Iago.

Hamlet was also offered on this first tour, but Salvini's bold and physical interpretation of the contemplative prince did not arouse much enthusiasm. The rest of his repertoire, all modern works, was less successful still. This pattern, established in New York, was repeated as Salvini toured the cities of the East and went inland to Chicago and south to New Orleans and Havana, following essentially the same route as Ristori six years before. His *Othello* played everywhere to overflowing houses and critical acclaim, but the rest of his repertoire attracted only the cultural elite and, in cities with large Italian populations, his cultural fellow countrymen. In all, he gave somewhat less than half the number of performances Ristori had given and gained only about one-third the income. The *New York Times* reported at the conclusion of the tour that once Grau had paid the actors and covered other expenses he had gained nothing at all for himself.[5] In any case Grau's profits were sufficiently small that, though he arranged for a return tour by Ristori, he did not invite Salvini again.

From the United States Salvini returned to South America, then to Paris, where he was contacted by the British impresario James Mapleson, who offered him an engagement for the spring of 1875 at Drury Lane itself. Salvini was well aware of the presumption of offering Shakespeare in a foreign tongue in the theatre which was more than any other in the world associated with the production of that dramatist, but the challenge overcame his misgivings and he returned to Italy to assemble a company.

In fact the Drury Lane of the 1870s was anything but the citadel of Shakespeare which it had been for many generations. The abolishment of the monopoly of the patent houses in 1843 had opened the Shakespeare canon to every London theatre. Covent Garden soon after switched permanently to opera and Drury Lane survived the new competition by mounting an erratic mixture of traditional drama, opera, ballet, melodrama, pantomime, circus acts—anything which might attract an audience. During these years Mapleson began to serve the theatre as the agent for the importing of Italian operatic stars. In 1863 a new manager, F. B. Chatterton, attempted, with modest success, to restore the name of Shakespeare to the bills of Drury Lane, though he still was forced to rely heavily on spectacular pantomimes, acrobatic acts, and variety entertainment as well. He presented more Shakespeare than any director of Drury Lane had done for twenty years, but he is doubtless best remembered for his bitter epigram: "Shakespeare spells ruin and Byron bankruptcy."

When Mapleson contacted Salvini in Paris and asked him to perform *Hamlet* and *Othello* for Chatterton, therefore, this did not probably reflect an interest in bringing more Shakespeare to Drury Lane. It was much more likely an attempt to appeal to the London public's thirst for theatrical novelty of any sort, though the opportunity to do this by means of Shakespeare doubtless intrigued Chatterton. Moreover he had already had some success with the importation of Italian singers and, like Grau in America, moved naturally to the further experiment of importing Italian actors.

For his London season Salvini selected a much more limited repertoire than he had offered in America, concentrating on *Othello*, which he gave thirty-four times. *Hamlet* was presented nine times and a modern drama, *The Gladiator*, four. His success with critics and general public was distinctly less qualified than it had been in America; older theatregoers compared his triumph to those of Kean and Rachel. His *Hamlet*, indifferently received in America, won warm praise from English critics. George Henry Lewes, who felt that no stage Hamlet could approach the vision of Shakespeare, nevertheless conceded that Salvini's Hamlet was the "least disappointing" he had ever seen, and the one containing the "most excellences."[6] Browning, long an admirer of Salvini, sent him a note expressing his delight in a performance in which "the entire lyre of tragedy sounded magnificently."[7] William Poel, the great reformer of Shakespearian staging, judged Salvini's *Hamlet* "the only perfect one within living memory" and later reported that these Salvini performances of 1875 were the stimulus which caused him to devote his life to the theatre.[8]

After this success Mapleson arranged with Salvini for a more ambitious tour the following year to Newcastle, Manchester, Liverpool, Edinburgh, Glasgow, Dublin, Belfast, and Birmingham as well as London. He was, however, unable to arrange for Salvini to return to Drury Lane. Chatterton clearly felt that the triumph in 1875 was due in significant measure to Salvini's novelty, and rather than repeat this offering and run the risk of sating the public's interest, he made his own arrangements to bring a new Italian star, Rossi, to Drury Lane the following season. Mapleson was thus forced to rent for Salvini the distinctly less prestigious and less well-located Queen's Theatre. Here Salvini gave seven performances of *Othello* in two weeks to respectable but not large houses. A revival of *Hamlet* and a new production of *Macbeth* were planned for the third week, but that Monday Mapleson announced that due to illness Salvini would be forced to cancel the remainder of his tour. In his autobiography Salvini gives convincing details of this illness,[9] but malicious critics were not lacking at the time who suggested that the combination of his indifferent reception at the Queen's and the simultaneous highly successful Shakespearian performances of Rossi at Drury Lane discouraged Salvini from extending the unequal contest by mounting anything beyond *Othello*.

Salvini was back in Florence in the spring of 1880 after touring through Austria, Germany, France, and Eastern Europe when he was contacted by Chizzola, now representing John Stetson, owner of the Globe Theatre in Boston. He proposed a second American tour, but with a strikingly different arrangement from the first. This time, instead of Salvini assembling a company of actors in Italy and bringing the entire troupe to America, Chizzola proposed that the star come alone and perform in Italian with a supporting company of American actors performing in English. At first, Salvini reports, he felt Chizzola had lost his reason or was playing a joke, but he gradually came to consider the idea more seriously. The entrepreneur argued that under these conditions audiences would find Salvini himself more comprehensible and would therefore receive him with greater enthusiasm than he had experienced on his first tour. As for possible problems in cuing, the actors should be easily able to memorize the final words of each of Salvini's speeches so as to come in at the proper point.[10] With no little misgiving, Salvini signed a contract pledging him to be in New York on 15 November 1880 to meet the actors with whom he would open in a bilingual *Othello* in Philadelphia just two weeks later.

Salvini received little encouragement from his friends either in Italy or America for this project; almost without exception they feared so bizarre an experiment doomed to catastrophe. Neither the actor nor his correspondents seem to have been aware that he was not the first to attempt something of the kind, though the example of his predecessor would not have done much in any case to raise his hopes. Fourteen years before, the noted German actor Bogumil Dawison had presented *Hamlet* in New York with a German company and then, as a sort of curiosity, offered *Othello* with Edwin Booth playing Iago. Dawison had spoken German, Booth and the supporting company English, and a Madame Schiller, playing Desdemona, had spoken German to Dawison and English to everyone else. This strange experiment aroused little enthusiasm and seems to have been mercifully forgotten long before the Salvini tour established the bilingual performance as a significant part of the age of the international star.

When Salvini first met his American company he was delighted to find that they had already been rehearsing for several weeks and were quite secure in their lines without a prompter—a marked improvement on the Italian actors of his experience. The first scene went very smoothly, but before long Salvini found himself becoming hopelessly lost amid the incomprehensible cues. Finally he had to resort to numbering his lines and simply repeating them in sequence to keep himself on the track. Under these conditions, the play proceeded fairly smoothly, and in time Salvini had become familiar enough with the lines of his American colleagues that he could even detect the substitution of a word. So he came gradually to recognize the words of Shakespeare's text, without any understanding of the English language itself.[11]

When the tour began in Philadelphia, the critic of the *Public Ledger* showed a certain ambivalence concerning the mixing of languages: "The effect was not the failure that had been anticipated by many playgoers," he reported, "though the company labored under a great disadvantage in being deprived of familiar cues." In summation, the reviewer felt that "if the play had been rendered entirely in English, it would have been the unanimous verdict that it was the greatest *Othello* ever heard by this generation, and with all its drawbacks, perhaps, it is still the greatest."[12]

As Stetson had hoped, this experiment generally proved much more attractive than Salvini's earlier, purely Italian performances in America, though the mixture of tongues was not without problems, especially early in the tour. Entrances were missed when actors did not recognize their cues in Italian, and in Boston Rosencrantz and Guildenstern got out of phase with Hamlet and found themselves out of lines before he reached the end of a scene. The *New York Times* of 14 December 1880 considered the experiment "less incoherent and absurd than one might have supposed it to be, but it was a discordant effect at best, and Mr. John Stetson's ingenious experiment will not, it is to be hoped, be imitated by other managers." The *New York World* of the same date echoed these sentiments, considering the effect "neither artistic nor agreeable." Complaints of this sort continued to be voiced throughout the tour, but they were balanced by comments from viewers who felt that the mingling of tongues was at most only a minor problem confined to the opening scenes. Thus the *St. Louis Globe-Democrat* reported that:

> it does not take long to wear the edge of novelty off the arrangement, and after the first scene, the auditor grows accustomed to it and even lapses into an intuitive sort of comprehension of the musical sentences that roll so magnificently from the tongue of the tragedian.[13]

The territory covered on this tour was essentially the same as before—the cities of the Northeast, Chicago, and New Orleans—and the repertoire almost the same—*Othello* and *Hamlet* along with several modern works—plus a new production of *Macbeth*. Only a few more than half as many performances were given this time (eighty-six in all), yet public enthusiasm was so much higher in 1880–81 that the tour's total income was higher than before and Salvini remained for a supplementary series of performances in New York, Washington, and Baltimore. This time there was no doubt that he would be invited to return again to America. The bilingual performance, with all its difficulties, had also been demonstrated to be commercially successful. Salvini was asked in Cincinnati if he foresaw other stars undertaking bilingual tours. He thought it unlikely, considering "the strain in concentration and thought" on the leading player. "I am the first artist who has essayed a long series of bilingual performances," he concluded, "and I think I shall be the last."[14] Yet before the year was out this prediction was proven mistaken. Rossi arrived in Boston to spend the season of 1881–82 following Salvini's example, even to the extent of using many of the same supporting actors.

For his next tour to America, in 1882–83, Salvini decided to prepare a major new Shakespearian work, and spent the spring and summer of 1882 in Florence working on *King Lear*. Although he opened the new season in New York, he first offered *Lear* at Boston's Globe Theatre, which was again serving as his sponsor and providing most of his supporting company. His interpretation was well received and drew extra praise through comparisons with Rossi's unsuccessful attempt at the same role the previous season. At the end of 1882 Salvini toured west to Chicago and St. Louis, returned to Boston in January of 1883, then went south to Philadelphia, Washington, and back again to New York, west again to Chicago (but playing to different cities on the way), and finally back to Boston in April to complete the tour. He gave 110 performances on this tour, his most successful yet. An extra boost was given to the latter part of the season by the appearance of the popular actress Clara Morris with his company, though unhappily she did not lend her talents to any of Salvini's Shakespearian plays, where he was generally rather weakly supported. Another spur to audiences was the persistent and quite false rumor (not at all discouraged by Salvini's sponsors) that the star was planning to give up international travelling and that this would be America's final opportunity to view him.

On the contrary, though Salvini deplored the exhausting travel and tight scheduling of the American tours, he now looked to this country as a place where he could offer productions too ambitious and demanding for the Italian stage. This was clearly the case with *Coriolanus*, which he began to prepare in 1883 as soon as he returned to Florence. He apparently never even considered offering this work on the Italian stage, for, as he explained, "it demands too costly a stage setting, and it was impossible to secure in the great number of assistants that artistic discipline without which the grandiose easily merges in the ridiculous."[15]

In 1884 Salvini was invited again to London, this time to

Covent Garden, but conditions there were not favorable to so costly an undertaking as *Coriolanus*. The failing administration of Ernest Gye was now in its final season, and Salvini was surely invited as a last, rather desperate, gamble by an administration on the brink of financial disaster. Salvini suggested some bilingual productions, but Rossi had already given London its first experience of this two seasons before, with so little success that Salvini was discouraged from taking the risk. He therefore appeared in London as he had done before, with a supporting Italian company and with a repertoire dominated, as always, by *Othello*. Once again he appeared not only in London but in the major cities of England, Scotland, and Ireland.

Back in a major London theatre, Salvini was more successful than he had been in 1876 at the Queen's, but he never rekindled the enthusiasm of his first London visit. His *Othello* was warmly praised, as always, but his *King Lear* and *Macbeth*, now seen in England for the first time, were considered to contain few new insights, and his supporting actors and staging were felt to be much inferior to what Irving had brought London audiences to expect in Shakespearian production. Audiences were generally small, perhaps because interest in Salvini had waned, or perhaps because the failing conditions at Covent Garden discouraged their attendance. Salvini complained in vain about the defective heating arrangements in the theatre, which forced the audience to sit in overcoats and furs and him to play with his teeth chattering from the cold.

It must have been an enormous relief for him to leave these conditions for the opulence of New York's Metropolitan Opera House, where he opened in the fall of 1885, first with *Othello* and *King Lear* and then with the new production of *Coriolanus*. Salvini was praised, as usual, for his power, his natural quality, and his polish, though *Coriolanus* never rivalled in popularity the leading works of his previous seasons. The supporting company was not brilliant, but careful attention had been given to the staging of the crowd scenes, and this, at a time when the Meininger productions in Europe had drawn attention to such matters, stimulated much favorable comment. The 1885–86 tour was arranged as usual by Charles Chizzola, and was Salvini's most extensive. After traveling in the East from Boston to

Washington, he went west to Chicago and eventually to California, returning by way of Salt Lake City, Denver, Cincinnati, and Minneapolis. On alternate nights, when Salvini was not performing, his son Alexander appeared, usually in *Romeo and Juliet*, which was given entirely in English with the promising young actress Viola Allen playing Juliet. Minnie Maddern, later one of America's leading actresses, was also a member of this company. At the end of the tour Salvini repeated Dawison's experiment of twenty years before, offering *Othello* with Booth as Iago in an extremely successful production given three times each in Philadelphia, Boston, and Washington. In each city this was accompanied by a single performance of *Hamlet* with Booth in the leading role and Salvini as the ghost.

Even Salvini's powerful constitution began to show the strain of constant touring during this exhausting season. He suffered a great deal from cold and damp in the railway trip across the Rocky Mountains, and after his first two performances in San Francisco totally lost his voice and was forced to cancel almost an entire week of performances. This set off a long and bitter conflict with Chizzola over the profits from the trip, culminating in a lawsuit against the actor. According to Chizzola, Salvini originally agreed to play five times each week (normally on Monday, Tuesday, Thursday, Friday, and Saturday matinees) and receive thirty-five per cent of the total receipts. Chizzola was to receive the rest and pay all expenses for the supporting company and incidentals. Tension first arose over the repertoire, since Chizzola argued that *Othello* was certain to be Salvini's most popular offering and therefore should be given at every opportunity. In fact Salvini, who liked to vary his repertoire and who found the playing of *Othello* in any case an enormous strain, gave it only thirty-three times out of over a hundred performances. When the tour was completed, Chizzola was furious to find that the *Othello* performances had received just over $46,000 while all others combined, more than twice as many performances, had brought in only $66,000. The entrepreneur, who had been arguing with Salvini about the contract ever since San Francisco, sued him for the difference in averages, which he claimed as a loss caused by Salvini. He also claimed damages for the performances missed in California and for eight other weeks when Salvini had given only four performances instead of the five Chizzola expected. As a final touch, he demanded $140 in payment for candles, claiming that Salvini had demanded four per evening and then kept them.[16]

This suit was still pending when Salvini left for Italy, and Chizzola soon despaired of ever collecting it. Indeed the Salvini tour, with all its dissapointments for him, was his last venture as an entrepreneur. He retired from the business and not long after left America to spend his remaining years in Paris. Salvini too would surely have been justified in making this fourth trip to America his last, considering the exhausting scheduling and the financial quarrels with which it ended. Yet the country for all its difficulties continued to lure him. In his memoirs the actor himself expresses some wonder at this, as he found himself preparing in 1889 to depart on this arduous undertaking once again:

> The actor's life in North America can be summed up in three words, "theatre, railroad, hotel." Very few are the cities in which a stop of two or three weeks is made. Away from the large centers, sometimes theatre and town are changed every night, with the intervening weariness of packing and sleeping-cars. And in addition there is the infliction of reporters, to which you must submit, the thousands of autographs from which there is no relief, and the admirers who persecute you. As you can imagine, at the end of such a season of seven months the actor is very eager to tear this shirt of Nessus from his back. But with all that, if I had been ten years younger I should have ventured thither ten times more.[17]

So in the fall of 1889 Salvini returned for the fifth and final time to America, this time under the sponsorship of the New York entrepreneur A. M. Palmer. Palmer, collecting his attractions for the new season during the summer of 1889, visited Salvini in Florence and set up the conditions for the tour. Once again Salvini would appear with American actors, though with no major new play. The one novelty of this tour would be an English version of *Samson*, which Salvini had performed in Italian during his first tour. The translation was to be made by

William Dean Howells, who had already furnished plays to Palmer's theatre. Salvini was to perform four times each week, on Monday, Wednesday, and Friday evenings, with a Saturday matinee. His son Alexander, now settled in America, would direct and occasionally perform on the remaining nights.

Alexander began rehearsing the American company on September 9 and his father arrived three weeks later to join in a final two rehearsals of each play before opening with *Samson* at Palmer's theatre on October 10. *Othello* was the only Shakespearian play presented on this tour and, as on Salvini's last tour, was offered for about one-third of the American performances. The tour was about the same length as that of 1885–86, but less extensive geographically. Salvini covered the major cities of the Eastern seaboard, ranged as far inland as Chicago, Minneapolis, and Omaha, and as far south as Richmond. He bade his farewell to the American people in the press, expressing his regret at taking this final leave of them. He was somewhat chagrined to find that this device had been so often abused by touring artists that it was widely assumed that, despite his seventy years, the artist would surely return to America again. In fact, though Salvini lived for another twenty-five years, he was now very near the end of his professional career. During the season of 1890–91 he gave his last major appearance in Italy and one of his last anywhere. Appropriately enough, this was in his home city of Florence, and the play given was *Othello*. For this final appearance the most famous Othello of his time and, in the opinion of many, the greatest Othello that had ever appeared on the stage took for the first and only time in his long career the role of Othello's nemesis, Iago.

5

Salvini's *Othello*

Salvini's *Othello* is easily the most thoroughly documented interpretation of any offered by the Italian touring stars. Presented hundreds of times in England and America, it was the subject of countless reviews and articles as well as of one full-length book, Edward Tuckerman Mason's *The Othello of Tommaso Salvini* (New York: Putnam's, 1890). Total reconstruction of any historical performance is of course impossible, but we can probably come as close to a moment-by-moment idea of how Salvini played Othello as we can to any great role of which we have only written records. The task is greatly facilitated by the fact that Salvini changed his delivery of the role very little over the years. His supporting players, different with each tour, were expected to adjust themselves to him as the star, and to require no adjustment from him in return. Thus we find that specific gestures, movements, and line readings remained remarkably consistent over a period of almost twenty years of touring. Evidence of this appears throughout the reviews and is occasionally specifically remarked upon.[1]

This allowed a careful observer like Mason to put together impressions from several tours, adding in new details each time he witnessed the performance. He began taking notes in the spring of 1881, saw *Othello* several more times during the next spring, and in the fall of 1882 drew together these notes to send to Salvini for adjustments or comments. In the autumn of 1889 he witnessed the play several more times, adding details to his earlier manuscript, and before making his final draft went to three performances early in 1890. During this ten-year span, covering all but Salvini's first American tour, Mason observed only a few minor changes in the interpretation, duly noted in his book. The following reconstruction naturally draws heavily upon his, supplemented with more specific details from other reviewers.

The first scene of Shakespeare's *Othello* was omitted by Salvini, possibly because it had proven so unfortunate for his mentor, Modena, but more likely because his production, like Ristori's *Macbeth*, was designed to focus upon the star, who should therefore be brought on stage as soon as possible and kept there through most of the evening. Salvini on his first entrance made a magnificent impression. He was a tall, powerfully built man, and in gorgeous Moorish dress with scarlet tarboosh, white turban, and white burnoose he was nearly overwhelming. Henry James thus described this first impression:

> His powerful, active, manly frame, his noble, serious, vividly expressive face, his splendid smile, his Italian eye, his superb, voluminous voice, his carriage, his tone, his ease, the assurance he instantly gives that he holds the whole part in his hands and can make of it exactly what he chooses,—all this descends upon the spectator's mind with a richness which immediately converts attention into faith, and expectation into sympathy. He is a magnificent creature, and you are already on his side.[2]

Salvini considered Othello to be a native of North Africa, and modeled his character upon a striking Moor he once saw at Gibraltar with a powerful physique, majestic walk, Roman face, and copper complexion. All of his costumes were taken from Venetian paintings of the fifteenth century depicting Moorish officers. The first words he spoke "assert a powerful charm" according to the *London Spectator:*

> His voice is surprisingly beautiful; flexible beyond belief; so full of musical inflexions, of change, of passion, of ten-

derness and of tears, that it translates its utterances, and makes the missing-out of the pathos and finesses of the original truly lamentable. His articulation is so distinct that every word is heard with ease in the most distant parts of the theatre, and not the least effort attends his most passionate outbursts.[3]

Salvini at once began to give evidence of the remarkable power of this admirable voice and physical presence to reinforce the content of his lines. The *Saturday Review* of 10 April 1875 spoke enthusiastically of his bearing: "that of a man long accustomed to the dignity of command," and the "certain swing of freedom in his walk," which conveyed a memory of the Moor's former "unhoused free condition." Indeed the shading of voice and gesture gave to this line a particular tonality so that the memory of his previous life seemed to possess him for a moment even as he spoke of the love which had banished it. He greeted Brabantio and his armed followers with an admirable quiet dignity, and his "Keep up your bright swords" was delivered in a voice that enforced obedience, followed by a pause, then a smile and a gentle "for the dew will rust them," striking almost a tender note and demonstrating the ease and confidence with which Othello held his authority. The reading of this line frequently sent a ripple of admiration through the audience. Salvini dominated the scene both physically and vocally, remaining up center, between the opposing parties, and by an imperious gesture keeping them apart on the line "Hold your hands." When the party of Brabantio left, Iago leaped forward as if to attack them, but was calmed by Othello's hand on his arm.

The scene in the Council Chamber of the Doge was Salvini's first major showpiece in the play. Even before he began to speak, during Brabantio's accusation, he drew all eyes to himself by the quiet dignity of his statuesque pose. His expression varied little as he regarded the old man with a look of growing wonder, occasionally darkened by a slight frown or impatient turn of the head as the attack became more bitter and personal. When Salvini at last began to speak, his manner contrasted sharply with Brabantio's. He first hesitated, as if seeking words

or pondering whether he should even respond to such outra-
geous charges. Then in a quiet, natural style, intense but devoid of rhetorical flourishes, he began his speech, standing
nobly as before with a cloak casually thrown over one arm.

The traditional English reading of these lines suggested the
trained orator, carefully arranging his effects, or, in more relaxed interpretations, a self-composed and reasoning man
calmly making a special plea on a rather formal occasion. Salvini departed from either of these approaches, taking the line
"Rude am I in speech" as a fact, not a rhetorical point, and
depended on the color of emotion and the natural music of his
marvelous voice to make the speech effective and moving. He
paused to reflect or remember; he groped for the proper word;
he struggled to subdue and channel his physical energy into
speech with the air of a man not accustomed to this task. The
result was not only an original reading, but a highly moving
one. "Audiences and actors alike gazed on him with undis-
guised admiration and drinking his words in eagerly," reported
the *Boston Globe* of 14 December 1880 "breaking out a moment
after he had finished into tumultuous and heartfelt applause."
So clear was his emotional expression that for most observers
the language barrier seems almost to have disappeared. According to the *New York World:*

> Had he spoke Greek or Choctaw it would have been much
> the same. There was that about him that was universal, and
> had he remained mute and contented himself with acting
> alone his audience could scarcely have failed to understand,
> so faithful was his portraiture of human instincts and their
> action.[4]

In his next long speech, Salvini began to add gesture and
movement to his already formidable skill in facial expression
and voice modulation. The wooing of Desdemona was re-
counted with the accompaniment of gestures of a particularly
illustrative kind. For "antres vast and deserts idle" he spread
his arms with a sweeping gesture; he pointed to the "hills,
whose heads touch heaven," turned aside with an expression
of horror and pushed away with both hands the image of the

"Cannibals that each other eat," and suggested the appearance of the "men whose heads do grow beneath their shoulders" by touching his own head with both hands and then lowering them to his breast. These tales completed, he returned to his method of unadorned narration until he came to the lines repeating Desdemona's words: " 'twas strange, 'twas passing strange. . . ." Here he began to impersonate Desdemona, speaking in a feminine tone and progressing from a rush of enthusiasm to the low, bashful, half-whispered "and that would woo her." This allowed him to make a striking contrast by returning to his own voice, charged with joy, for "Upon this hint I spoke."

Salvini observed the arrival of Desdemona with a look of the deepest tenderness and listened to her narration beaming with happiness. His "sublime trust" and "almost boyish affection," said the *Boston Globe* of 27 November 1873 "was superbly conceived and as superbly manifested." Nothing is anywhere reported of Desdemona's reading of this important line, nor is this particularly surprising. Audiences and reviewers alike were concentrating on the reactions of Salvini, the star of the production, as they were expected to do. This required that Salvini's reactions to the speeches of others be as complex and specific as the gestures and expressions which he used to support his own lines. An example may be seen during Brabantio's line giving up his daughter to Othello:

> *Brabantio:* Come hither, Moor (Salvini crosses to him and stands gravely attentive, hand on breast). I here do give thee that with all my heart, (Salvini beams with delight, bends forward, extends his right hand and utters a low sound of gratitude and affection) which, but thou hast already (Salvini draws back, frowning) with all my heart I would keep from thee (Salvini draws up to his full height, gazes at Brabantio in grief and anger, turns from him and stalks away).

Desdemona's plea to the Duke to be allowed to accompany her husband to Cyprus gave Salvini further opportunity to demonstrate by glance and facial expression his growing joy in her. At her line "Let me go with him," he rushed impulsively forward and lifted her from her knees, then began to embrace her and bent to kiss her forehead before suddenly recalling the formality of the occasion. He turned from her with a gesture of apology, and solemnly made his final plea to the Doge and Senators. As the Senators began to leave, Desdemona held out her arms to her father, but he spurned her and crossed to Othello to give him the warning "Look to her, Moor." Salvini showed Othello clearly staggered by this speech. He started backward with both arms raised, then, crying out "My life upon her faith," he rushed after the departing Brabantio as if he would attack him. At the rear of the stage he gained control of himself, returned to Desdemona and resumed the interrupted embrace. He then led her from the stage gazing rapturously into her face. This was the end of Salvini's first act, since the following Roderigo-Iago interchange was omitted.

The second act began as in Shakespeare, and the entrance of Othello was prepared by an elaborate bit of staging. A cannon was fired offstage and shouts and military music heard at a distance. As these became louder and closer, the stage began to fill with citizens of Cyprus, soldiers and sailors, waving their caps and cheering. At the height of the clamor, with a clash of cymbals and blare of trumpets, Othello appeared in full armor. This appearance, capped by Salvini's joyful hail to Desdemona, "O my fair warrior," invariably roused a storm of applause. The following lines to Desdemona echoed the tenderness of the first act, but added a degree of sensuousness and burning passion which Salvini would continue to develop as a key to his character. He avoided any suggestion of tragedy to come. Even the possible "fear" expressed at the end of this speech was swallowed up in the joy of the encounter. The lovers were locked in embrace during Iago's "O you are well tuned," and Salvini embraced Desdemona once again before exiting with her into the castle.

The following scenes between Iago and Roderigo and Iago and Cassio, culminating in the drunken fight, were retained, though much reduced in length. Nevertheless sufficient time passed before the alarm was sounded that some reviewers complained because Othello reappeared not in gown and slippers as English stage tradition demanded but still in full armor—chain, plate, helmet, gauntlets, and all. Aside from conjuring up visions of Othello retiring to bed in this panoply, his return in armor decreased the effect of his breaking up the duel by the sheer force of his authority and allowed little suggestion of his having been interrupted in a tender moment with his new bride. After 1875 Salvini heeded these criticisms and entered in soft robes with a loose cloak, which he later wrapped tenderly about Desdemona when she appeared.

The solicitude Salvini expressed for Desdemona was played in sharp contrast to his anger with Cassio. There was not a hint of sadness and disappointment in his lieutenant, points generally made by English Othellos; even the line "I loved thee, Cassio" was delivered without a trace of recognition of past comradeship. The *New York Tribune* was so disturbed by this lack of compassion that, in its review of 20 February 1883, it complained that this "had always been a blur upon Salvini's portraiture of Othello." Instead Salvini snarled at Cassio in wrath, shook his fist in his face on "I'll make thee an example," and dismissed him with contempt and scorn. The focus of the scene was clearly upon the relationship between Othello and Desdemona, and Desdemona's appearance was the occasion for a marked increase in Othello's fury at the offending officer.

The two brief scenes opening the traditional third act were omitted in Salvini's version, so that the act began with Cassio's conversation with Desdemona in scene 3. During this act Salvini built gradually from the calm assurance and almost uxorious passion of the opening acts to the bestial rage and blind fury of the close, and many spectators felt that this modulation, passing through many carefully indicated intermediate stages, was the finest achievement of his art. The opening interchange with Desdemona Salvini played in the same general tone of his earlier scenes with her, without a trace of suspicion or uneasiness. He looked offstage after Cassio and commented "I do believe 'twas he" without emotional overtones, and when Desdemona admitted that it was indeed the lieutenant, Salvini gave Iago a nod and smile as if to say "You see, I was right." He then sat at a table and began to write, giving Desdemona occasional smiles and half-mechanical answers until she knelt before him and took his pen on "Tomorrow dinner then?" He turned to watch her, still smiling, as she continued to plead, then interrupted her, with an impulsive embrace, as one might give a favorite child, on his "Prithee no more: let him come when he will." A slightly graver note was struck on Desdemona's line "Why this is not a boon" and Othello's response "I will deny thee nothing," but immediately the playful affection returned on "Whereon, I do beseech thee." Before Desdemona left, Salvini gave her a final quick embrace and was about to add to it a kiss when his eye lit upon Iago and Emilia and he modestly refrained. The entire scene was very lightly played and was cited by Mason as a good example of one of the outstanding and almost unique features of Salvini's art: the introduction of exquisite high-comedy effects into passages where no other tragedian of the period would have considered using them.

After his wife had departed, Othello assumed a businesslike air and returned to his papers. The new scene began in silence, like a tableau, with Othello seated quietly at his desk, in a casual blue jacket and trousers, the light from a window to his right accentuating the crisply curled hair which was set close about his dark face and throat. He looked, reported one observer, like a portrait by Titian.[5] This quiet opening provided a basis and a contrast for the display of passion which was soon to follow. After Othello had written for a moment, Iago spoke, and Othello paused, irritated at being again interrupted. This note of irritation he continued until Iago's laconic "indeed." Salvini repeated the "indeed" ironically, then turned, pen in hand, to look at his companion for the first time. He then repeated the "indeed" as an emphatic restatement of his own, but the poison had begun to work. The first step from the assured lover of the opening acts to the revengeful monster of the catastrophe was thus taken.

Iago's "Think my lord" caused Othello his first clear uneasiness. He threw down his pen and crossed to Iago to say "Thou dost mean something." His whole attention was now riveted on penetrating Iago's veiled references. After Iago's line "Why, then, I think Cassio's an honest man," Salvini, standing beside him, looked long and searchingly into his eyes, then smiled, shook his head, and moved away with a slight wave of the hand as if to urge Iago to speak frankly. An impatience with his companion's reticence seemed Salvini's main reaction during the following lines. He seemed to acknowledge no relation to himself in the comments about jealousy and his disclaimer, "No; to be once in doubt / Is once to be resolved," seemed open and sincere. This self-assurance, however, rapidly faded, and after Iago's "Look to your wife" Salvini seemed to struggle in vain against a growing doubt and apprehension. The lines "Dost thou say so?" and "And so she did" diminished in volume to become scarcely audible. His concern now appeared to be largely to hide his emotional upheaval from Iago. He refused to face his tormentor, spoke in low tones ("Not a jot, not a jot" became simply an inarticulate sound of suffering) and finally crossed to a large window stage right and stood looking up at the sky. Twice his disturbance seemed on the brink of erupting into physical violence, on:

> He thought 'twas witchcraft—but I am much to blame
> I humbly do beseech you of your pardon
> For too much loving you . . .

and

> Foh! one may smell in such, a will most rank,
> Foul disproportion, thoughts unnatural,
> But pardon me: I do not in position
> Distinctly speak of her . . .

Each time Othello's hand sought his sword and Iago, sensing the danger, drew back. The *Boston Globe* of 27 November 1873 felt that Salvini's play of conflicting emotions in this scene "was conceived with indescribable power in gesture and facial play." This reviewer found particularly masterly Salvini's playing of the moment when Othello requests Iago to set on his wife to observe Desdemona: "He hesitates as though ashamed of the meanness to which he is about to stoop, and then, with his eyes cast down and in a low voice, he slowly stammers out his pitiable proposal."

Afterward, with Iago dismissed, Salvini could show the full working of the poison. He tried in vain to return to his writing and after several frustrated attempts dashed the pen to the table, struck the table with his fist, and began to pace the chamber in agitation. The brief scene with Desdemona provided only a pause in the mounting Othello-Iago tension. Her appearance seemed to bring Othello briefly back to himself, and his "I'll not believe 't" Salvini delivered with grim conviction downstage and full front, with a shake of the head and a raised, clenched fist. Yet the effects of the doubt prevented him from looking directly at her during this scene, or from speaking above a low, faint tone. On this same low, dejected note Salvini began the next scene with Iago, following the brief handkerchief scene between Iago and Emilia.

The climax of the psychological duel between Othello and Iago was one of the most celebrated scenes in Salvini's production. The farewell to his former occupation he delivered with great pathos, sunk in his chair and turned from Iago. He leaped to his feet on "O you mortal engines," then fell back into the chair for "Othello's occupation's gone!," which was followed by passionate sobbing, his head bent over the table resting on his outstretched arms. After a long pause, Iago spoke quietly: "Is't possible, my lord?" Salvini then gradually recovered, first sitting upright and convulsively grasping the arms of his chair, shaking his head and muttering "Villain," then raising his voice gradually until he leaped from the chair and with a roar rushed upon his tormentor. The *New York World* described the effect of this carefully prepared attack, noting that Salvini

needed no words to depict the struggling and contrary emotions that possessed him; the burning desire to know all; the hope that all was nothing; the conviction that it was guiltiness most damnable and yet that he could not bear the utterance. All this was so plainly marked in his action and was withal so exciting that the audience at times almost rose to its feet. The house was swept along by the expresson of burning passion it witnessed, and so finely was the culmination graduated that when Othello seized Iago by the throat at the lines which in English are "Be sure of it . . . then answer my awakened wrath!"—the pent-up feelings of the auditors let themselves loose in one long and spontaneous roar of applause.[6]

Yet even now Salvini had not reached the peak of his emotional build. Still grasping Iago by the throat, at times seeming almost to twist his head from his body, and threatening him with his clenched right hand, Salvini began on "For nothing canst thou to damnation add" to twist him violently from left to right, then finally to fling him prostrate to the floor. With clenched fists raised to heaven, eyes rolling, and features contorted with rage he raised one foot as if to stamp out Iago's life. The *Boston Globe* called it

> the most terrifically realistic piece of acting ever seen. The audience half rose from their seats and a suppressed cry rang through the house, which, accompanied by a shriek of affright uttered by Iago, seemed to recall Othello to himself. He appeared to gather himself together by a supreme effort of the will, and gently raising the prostrate Iago, he staggered to an ottoman at the back of the scene, and there lay panting with emotion for several minutes until the uproar of acclamation caused by this thrilling scene had abated.[7]

During the remainder of the scene, Salvini seemed constantly on the brink of allowing this animal fury to burst forth once more, managing only with the greatest effort to hold it in check. His "Death and damnation! O!" was like the cry of a wounded wild beast, but it was followed immediately by a visible bracing of his body, and a grim, death-like smile as he seated himself at the table to hear Iago's story. As this story continued he writhed in the chair as if on a machine of torture, grasping the arms and then seizing the cloth upon the table and crumpling it in his fist. Again his anguish burst forth in words; "Now do I see 'tis time" was like the cry of a man suddenly pierced by a sword thrust. The line "O, blood, blood, blood" was another cry of rage and suffering. Then came an abrupt shift in tone and a striking effect. Observed the *Chicago Tribune* (14 December 1880): "Those who noticed last night the pause before the utterance of 'Like to the Pontic sea,'—as if the

Oriental imagination were struggling through a brain suffused with black blood, to find some image broad and terrible enough to express its deadly purpose—saw the perfection of dramatic art." At the conclusion of this speech Salvini dropped to his knees and extended his arms upward to swear his oath of vengeance. As Iago knelt beside him to swear in turn, Salvini watched him with a horrible intensity, panting heavily, his mouth stretched open and his tongue visible and curled. A final passionate outburst came on Othello's response to Iago's "But let her live"—"Damn her, lewd minx! O, damn her," rendered in Italian as "Oh! dannata, dannata, la cortigiana vile!" Salvini gave the "Oh" as a cry of passionate protest to Iago's advice, then approached Iago and, emphasizing the word with clenched fist, cried "Dann*a*ta, dann*a*ta" in intense hatred.

Henry James said the last two acts of Salvini's *Othello* represented "the finest piece of tragic acting that I know,"[8] and certainly Salvini here displayed the full force of his artistic power. His fourth act began with the traditional act 3, scene 4, omitting the brief opening sequence with the clown. The intensity of his suppressed emotion, already well established in the preceding scene with Iago, continued through the sequence in which Othello questioned Desdemona about the handkerchief. By forced smiles, deep sighs, agonized pauses, and abrupt shifts in tone Salvini clearly indicated the effort of holding in check an almost unendurable passion. The intensity of the scene gradually increased as Desdemona approached Othello, pleading for Cassio, and he continued to repeat "The handkerchief" with increasing vehemence and bitter irony. On "In sooth, you are to blame," Desdemona threw her arms about his neck, only to be violently thrust back with repulsion and hatred on his "Away!" Salvini's exit here involved a complicated piece of pantomime. He retreated backward from Desdemona as she sank weeping into a chair. He then turned to catch sight of Emilia, whom he had forgotten in his passion, and of the rejected handkerchief which he had thrown to the floor. Pointing to it, he took a few steps toward Emilia, saying "Ah—" as if he would question her further about it. Then he paused, shook his head and turning full front to the audience, gazed at both women with a sidelong frown of anger, uttered a scornful exclamation and then strode from the room, shaking his bowed head and muttering deeply and darkly, in a sound like distant thunder. The scene ended soon after, since the brief entrance of Cassio and Iago into the room was cut and Desdemona and Emilia's reactions to Othello's anger reduced to a few speeches.

The Cassio-Bianca scene ending act 3 was also cut; indeed, Bianca did not appear in Salvini's version at all, and Cassio was deprived of almost all individuality. The next scene was thus the opening of the traditional fourth act, the further baiting of Othello by Iago. Iago's more crudely sexual lines were not cut, as they commonly were in English productions of the period, but they were laundered by the Italian translator. Thus the Italian version of the line "Or to be naked with her friend a-bed" became "Or to be with her friend alone," and "Lie—" "With her?" "With her, on her; what you will" became "With her?" "With her, in her chamber, what you will." Salvini, despite his flair for physical display, somewhat surprisingly omitted Othello's epileptic seizure. The long line leading up to the seizure was reduced by him to "He? With her? With her? O, infamy!" The last was uttered as an anguished cry, upon which Salvini turned from Iago and cast an agonized glance toward Desdemona's room; then, hiding his face with his arm and weeping aloud, he flung himself into the chair and once more buried his head in his arms on the table.

After Iago's line "Work on," there was a long cut, removing Cassio and the entire scene where Othello overhears the conversation between Iago and Cassio. Othello's line "My heart is turned to stone" was thus delivered in Salvini's version not as a response to the Iago-Cassio scene but as a line of recovery from the outburst of weeping at the table. The scene of the arrival of Lodovico from Venice containing Othello's attack on his wife, normally cut in English productions, was retained by Salvini and caused a great sensation. The *Boston Globe* called it

> almost too exacting in the demands it made upon the feelings. The rapid changes of facial expression, when his attention is divided between the letter from the Senate and Desdemona, when he attempts to preserve an outward calm and dignity towards the messengers, while he overwhelms his

wife with contempt and insult, were astounding in the effect
they produced.[9]

The lines immediately before the blow were adjusted so that
Salvini had only a series of short speeches to deliver. He gave
them so rapidly that they seemed part of a continuous line,
oblivious of Desdemona's responses and building emotionally
to the blow:

Othello: Fire and brimstone!
Desdemona: My lord?
Othello: Are you wise? Now who would say it?
Desdemona: Say what?
Othello: Indeed!
Desdemona: Why, sweet Othello—
Othello: Devil!

Here he struck her on the side of the head, not with his hand
but with the letter, then turned aside, weeping in shame and
sorrow. Mastering himself, he returned to respond to Lodovico
in a tone of forced courtesy and bitter irony, maintained
through the rest of the interchange. Making his exit, he gave
Lodovico a wave of the hand, an obsequious bow, and a horrible smile. Mason noted that here as elsewhere Salvini achieved
a profoundly tragic effect by using laughter and smiles to suggest a suffering even deeper than what could be expressed by
tears and groans. He turned and took a few steps toward the
exit, whereupon the pent-up passion burst forth and he left the
stage with loud cries of anguish, wringing his hands above his
head.

The following scene (the traditional act 4, scene 2) Salvini
presented in transposed order, beginning just after the exit of
Othello with Emilia's line "Alas, what does this gentleman conceive" (which thus seemed to be referring to the public scene
with Lodovico and not to the private interview which followed), running to the end of Shakespeare's scene, with some
cuts, that is, through the conversations between Desdemona
and Iago and Roderigo and Iago. Then Salvini's version went
back to pick up the opening half of the scene, with Othello,
Desdemona, and Emilia. The effect of this transposition was to

allow the act to build toward a concluding scene dominated by the star. In this encounter Salvini continued to shift rapidly from bitter ironic humor to bursts of passionate rage to prostrate grief. "Salvini has a way of broadly filling the stage," observed Mary Clarke, "and occupying it by large and wide circles of motion, that admirably accord with the restlessness of jealousy and perturbed feeling," and she cited as an example this scene of reproach, when Salvini turned from the kneeling Desdemona "writhing, and went toward the farthermost depths of the stage, where, with his back to the audience, he sobbed forth the chief part of that bitter lamentation speech— 'Had it pleas'd Heaven to try me with affliction.' "[10]

The striking conclusion of this act visually recalled Othello's earlier departure from Lodovico. When Emilia reentered, Salvini knitted his fingers together, held his hands down, inclined his entire body and bent his head to smile at her with the most obsequious mock politeness. On "Here's gold for you," he took a purse from his girdle and jingled it before her. Emilia haughtily moved past him and he followed, thrusting the purse at her on "Keep our counsel." He then threw the purse onto a table, then looked at Emilia and laughed (that tortured laugh so much admired by Mason), picked it up again and roughly grasping her by the arm threw it at her feet. Motioning her to take it, he laughed again, loudly and bitterly, then turned to the door and rushed out with a loud cry of anguish, holding his hands above his head in that gesture of despair which he had led the audience to associate with his character. So ended Salvini's fourth act.

The final act began with the scene between Emilia and Desdemona which makes up most of the traditional act 4, scene 3, including Desdemona's Willow Song. In Salvini's version this scene flowed directly into act 5, scene 2. After Emilia left, Desdemona went upstage and opened the curtains to the bedalcove, dimly lighted from within. She entered the alcove, drawing the curtains closed and leaving the stage empty. After a long pause there was the muttering of distant thunder; then Othello entered to begin his line "It is the cause." The intervening scene, with the attack on Cassio and the stabbing of Roderigo, was omitted.

Salvini entered apparently determined to slay Desdemona at once, for, after a moment of meditation at the door, he threw his long red mantle upon a chair, drew his sword and moved decisively to the alcove. His first glimpse of the sleeping Desdemona blunted this purpose and he moved back downstage on "Yet I'll not shed her blood," laying his sword on the table firmly as he said "I'll *not*" (which in the Italian version ended the line). The line "Put out the light and then put out the light" was much more baldly rendered in Italian as "I shall put out this light and then your life." Salvini in fact never did the first; he moved to do so, then was distracted by the thought of Desdemona. Returning to the alcove for another look at her, he then returned downstage, his voice broken with tears, on "I must weep." His speech was interrupted by a flash of lightning and roar of thunder, drawing him to the window for the line "This sorrow's heavenly; it strikes where it doth love." Desdemona, apparently awakened by the thunder, appeared between the alcove curtains and, when Othello refused to turn toward her or even look at her, came downstage to where he was standing. Still he avoided her, moving upstage and pacing back and forth as he questioned her, like a caged wild beast. Indeed the image of the aroused tiger was regularly employed by critics describing this scene.

On Desdemona's "Alas, he is betray'd, and I undone!" the full fury of the beast burst forth and the following lines and actions proceeded headlong in uncontrolled frenzy. The *San Francisco Chronicle* thus described Salvini's transformation at this point:

> The stride of dignity which once carried him haughtily before the Senate becomes the stride of the wild beast, the body loses all its manliness, the face has changed until one does not see a feature of the Moor as he begins the play—the man, body and soul, is transformed.[11]

On "Out, strumpet, weep'st thou for him to my face?" Salvini dragged the kneeling Desdemona to her feet and in his first performances in America took her up bodily and carried her shrieking to the bed (the *New York Times* reported that he tucked her "under his arm as if she were an umbrella"). Subsequently he changed this action to another less overpowering, but perhaps more cruel. He grasped her by one arm and with the other seized her hair and bent back her head as if he would break her neck, then half carried, half dragged her, struggling and crying out, across the stage to the alcove. She was murdered behind the curtains, where her shrieks and groans, mingled with his hoarse cries and animal-like growls, indicated with painful clarity the act which was taking place.

Despite the horrifying realism of this death scene, Salvini was offended by critics who applied to it such terms as "barbaric," "passionate," or even "impulsive." To him it was a considered, inevitable, and even heroic act. He observed in a Roman journal in the early 1870s:

> Othello loves Desdemona and kills her because she is untrue to the laws of honor, and not for hate or jealousy; he gives satisfaction to honesty, which he believes soiled by the unhappy Desdemona. He does not inebriate himself with blood; he weeps because he is obliged to shed it, and is horror-struck by his crime. It is not his jealousy, it is not hate, it is not a ferocious impulse; it is the indignation of the honest man which impels the Moor to sacrifice his love, his adoration, his worship for Desdemona.[12]

In a later analysis of the character he suggested that Othello is forced to kill Desdemona by the demands of his loyalty and honor; "her death is a sacrifice which he owes to society; he has the right to inflict this punishment and has no thought of concealment."[13]

After the murder of Desdemona there was a long moment of silence; then the voice of Emilia was heard outside the chamber. Salvini emerged from the alcove, seemingly stunned by what had just occurred, and came slowly down to admit her. A touch of his fury returned as Emilia began to upbraid him for the murder. He seized his sword from the table, then immediately repented his impulse and sank down into a chair as she gave the alarm. The further speeches of Emilia gradually aroused him from his lethargy (these moved rapidly, with much cutting, omitting entirely Iago's attempt to stab her) until her "He begg'd of me to steal it," which brought Othello to his feet. Assured of the truth of Emilia's story, he started back with a loud cry; standing up center, facing full front, arms stretched heavenward and head thrown back, he roared out with the full power of his tremendous voice: "Are there no stones in heaven. . . ." Then, instead of running at Iago as Shakespeare's text suggests, he turned upstage and with cries of weeping and groaning threw himself down to embrace Desdemona's body.

George Henry Lewes, who claimed never to have witnessed anything "so musically perfect in the *tempo* and intonation, so emotionally perfect in the expression" as Salvini's third act confrontation with Iago, considered the fifth act "underfelt and overacted." In his opinion Salvini "alternately raged and blubbered—and was never pathetic. . . . His pathetic tones are not searching; there are no tears in his voice; instead of that he is unpleasantly tearful—which is a totally different thing."[14] Salvini responded to this criticism in an interview in the *New York Times*, casting his comments along the lines of the then-popular controversy over how much an actor really felt of his role:

> Tears do come sometimes in strongly emotional or pathetic scenes, but I try to control them. Real tears have no place on the stage. If I allowed them to get the better of me my voice would break and I should be of no good in my part. My aim is to move myself to the point where tears would naturally come, and then by my art to hold them in check.[15]

As Othello lay weeping, Lodovico ordered his attendants to seize Iago (who had not left the stage). Then, in what Henry James called an "ineffaceable" moment and "the high-water mark of dramatic experience", Salvini, on one knee beside Desdemona, regarded Iago for a "terrible moment" and then sprang into an avenging action "among the most poignant the actors' art has ever given us."[16] Giving a line only dimly related to Shakespeare's original:

> Is that a man?—His look poisons—his touch burns—his life is a lie.
> Oh, if thou art a devil, thou dost not fear death!

he rushed downstage, seizing Montano's sword from its scabbard as he passed him. He wounded Iago, who was then shielded from further harm by Lodovico and the attendants. On Iago's line "Demand me nothing," Othello gave up the pursuit, threw down the sword, and sank into his chair beside the table, where he remained for some moments, in James's words, "prostrate, panting, helpless, annihilated, convulsed with long inarticulate moans."[17] As Iago was being forced offstage by the attendants, Cassio entered, went upstage to look at Desdemona's body, then came down to speak to Othello:

> *Cassio:* Dear general, I never gave you cause.
> *Othello* (in a low tone): That's he that was Othello.
>   Give me your hand, your pardon.
>   (He clasps Cassio's hand without looking up.)
> *Lodovico:* O thou Othello, that wert once so good,
>   Fall'n in the practice of a damned slave,
>   What shall be said to thee?

After these truncated reactions, the others began to leave, until Othello's words stopped them. His pleading, "Soft you a word or two," they ignored, but some of his old tone of command returned in "I have done the state some service," and they paused then to hear him. He continued quietly, his words interrupted by weeping, until "their medicinal gum," when his eyes fell upon the scimitar which he had carried throughout the play and earlier left upon the table. Life and energy returned, and he rose to his feet, slapping the table with his hand as he said "Set you down this." He then moved rapidly and energetically toward the moment of his suicide. "The history of the stage does not record another such death," said the *Boston Globe.*

> This intense piece of realism at the end of the play which out-Zolas Zola, still remains, of course, the most exciting and thrilling portion of the great Italian's performance. It has become so identified with his reputation that it is the first thing brought to mind by the mention of his name.[18]

On "I took by the throat the circumcised dog," Salvini pantomimed this action in the air before him, standing center stage, and on "and smote him," flashed his scimitar through the air to destroy the imagary foe. Then he paused momentarily, steeling himself for the deed to come. After a glance at his companions he seized the point of the blade with his left hand, the hilt with his right, and crying out "thus," sawed it violently back and forth across his own throat, making a horrible gurgling noise in his throat as if blood and air were escaping, and dropping his head back as if half severed. He dropped the sword and staggered backward toward the bed to die near his beloved, but the death spasms overcame him before he reached this goal. Dropping to the floor, he rolled about with horrible twisting and contractions of his limbs as the curtain rapidly fell. The final image, concluded the *Boston Globe*, "produces a tension of the nerves from which it is not easy to recover."

The brutality of this scene naturally drew some complaint, especially since staging tradition called for a more decorous dagger thrust to the heart. Doubtless the possibility for display offered by Salvini's alternative constituted much of its appeal for him, but he defended his innovation on the more respectable grounds of historical veracity:

In the first place, this manner is more in accordance with the custom of the people of Africa, who usually execute their criminals and enemies in this way; then the arms used by these people are of a curved form, and, as such, are more adapted to this mode than to any other. . . . This form of suicide may indeed be opposed to tradition, but while I respect this authority, I cannot submit to it. I must, therefore, insist upon dying in my own way.[19]

6

Salvini's *Hamlet*

The *Hamlet* of Salvini drew much more negative critical reaction than his *Othello*. Partly, no doubt, this was due to a kind of Anglo-Saxon possessiveness about Hamlet not felt for the more "southern" Othello, but Salvini also stimulated protest by offering a version much further from the original than *Othello* had been. Many scenes and passages were, of course, traditionally cut for English presentation, and a few of these Salvini restored, but his omissions as a whole were serious enough to alter considerably the shape and flow of the play. There seems much justice in the charge that he presented only a portion of *Hamlet*, though one might argue over the significance or centrality of that portion. The first scene, with the appearance of the Ghost on the platform, was omitted entirely, and in the following court scene Voltemand and Cornelius were merely mentioned in passing. Thus the play essentially began with the King's first address to Hamlet. It was far from the impressive entrance which Salvini preferred to make; indeed his strong physical presence seemed to work against the quiet opening of this scene, as it did against the popular conception of Hamlet throughout the play. Salvini admits in his autobiography:

In the eyes of the public my form seemed too colossal for Hamlet. The adipose, lymphatic, and asthmatic thinker of

Shakespeare must change himself, according to the popular imagination, into a slender, romantic, and nervous figure.[1]

Salvini, on the other hand, as William Winter observed, even in the traditional black velvet tunic and hose of the melancholy prince, "looked like a gladiator."[2]

His opening line, also, was not calculated to raise the spirits of lovers of Shakespeare. "A little more than kin and less than kind" became in Italian (and in the English-language libretto sold in the theatre) "a little more than a cousin and less than a son." Not until the first soliloquy was Salvini able to make use of his striking voice and power of quiet natural delivery to create a significant impression. During the following interchange with Horatio and the guards, Salvini was able to add his ability at expressive gesture. Said *Century Magazine*:

> The airy grace of his action, which interprets his words to those who cannot understand his language, is strikingly apparent throughout the play. When Horatio related the visitation of the ghost, Salvini's gesture with which he accompanies the word *"Armato?"*—waving his hands from head to feet—is as eloquently descriptive of the mailed figure as Shakespeare's lines.[3]

Doubtless this made the action easier for non-Italians to follow, but Salvini's tendency to illustrate physically seems at times to have led him dangerously close to charade. For example he illustrated the line "In my mind's eye, Horatio" by pointing to his head on "mind" and his eye on "eye."

The following Polonius family scene was much cut, leaving only material necessary to fill in the background to the action. Hamlet's promise and enthusiasm in happier days were mentioned, and brother and father warned Ophelia to protect her honor, but Polonius's "few precepts" to his departing son disappeared entirely. The next scene, on the platform, suffered less and was generally accounted one of the outstanding sequences of the production (the others being the play scene and the interview in the Queen's chamber). The *Boston Globe* of 6 January 1881 found the innovation of introducing and dismissing the ghost through trapdoors "decidedly objectionable," but called Salvini's rendering of the scene "admirable, the most artistic feature of his performance being his attitude and expression of awestruck horror at his father's spirit." In his own commentary on the play, Salvini stressed the radical change in Hamlet after the encounter with the ghost. At the beginning the actor should assume "a dignified but sorrowful melancholy, inclining rather towards gentleness," but after meeting the ghost a "new Hamlet" should appear, bent on vengeance, his soul in distress, his nerves at high tension. As for the pivotal encounter:

> At the opening of the scene with the ghost, Hamlet should be violently excited; at the appearance of his father's spirit he should be seized with a terrible shuddering. When the mysterious form beckons to him, he should follow it as though impelled by a supernatural force. During the revelation of his uncle's crime, Hamlet should listen attentively, with veneration, as if almost afraid to move. The actor should make his audience realize the seriousness and gravity of such a scene. To my mind useless gestures, or walking up and down the stage for picturesque effect, would spoil the intensity of this beautiful scene.[4]

Descriptions of the scene generally support this analysis. At the first appearance of the specter, Salvini gave an impressive backward start of terror, but when he followed the ghost to another part of the platform, in the words of the *New York Herald* of 3 October 1873: "he turned his back upon that phantom with an easy grace and admirable reserve of nervous force." Actually, of course, he wanted to give the audience the benefit of a full-front representation of the play of emotions across his features as he heard the ghost's story. Most viewers were suitably impressed, but not the *Saturday Review*:

> A merely physical power of facial contortion is as little fitted for the portrayal of deep emotion as are the cries in falsetto to which the player here misapplies the resources of his voice.[5]

The sequence following the ghost's departure suffered greatly in Salvini's adaptation. The swearing scene with

Horatio and Marcellus was removed, together with the critical "antic disposition" speech, and replaced by a short scene between Hamlet and Horatio in which the Prince expressed nothing of the passion or self-imposed reticence of the original, but simply informed his friend that he had been told a horrible secret and was forbidden to reveal it. The ghost was allowed a final departing groan beneath the stage to provide Salvini with an effective closing gesture, thus reported by the *Boston Globe* of 3 October 1873: "Nothing could be more expressive or more touching than the caressing manner in which he extended his hands and murmured, in a tenderly imploring tone of voice, 'Rest, rest, perturbed spirit.'" Despite such gentle moments, the overwhelming impression given by Salvini during this first act was one of power and strong determination, which rather disturbed those who were accustomed to a less dynamic, more contemplative Hamlet. The *New York Times* of 3 October 1873 quoted, with approval, the remark of "a young gentleman seated near the stage" at the end of Salvini's first act: "Well, that fellow won't make much of sticking the King."

Salvini's second act began with the traditional act 2, scene 2, omitting the Reynaldo scene. The long and complex second scene was radically altered by cutting. After a few lines introducing Rosencrantz and Guildenstern, Polonius entered and revealed without preliminaries his suspicion of Hamlet's love for Ophelia. This removed the sequence of the return of the ambassadors as well as one of the play's best-loved passages, Polonius's exaggerated and comic delay before imparting his discovery. Perhaps out of respect for the presumed Nordic quality of *Hamlet*, Salvini seemed as determined to remove every trace of humor from this play and from his own character as he had been to find and emphasize light, even comic moments in *Othello*. His encounter with Polonius was thus reduced to a few lines, much to the regret of George Henry Lewes, who found these lines admirable and deplored "the mutilation of a text which reduced this aspect of Hamlet to a transient indication."[6] The sequence with Rosencrantz and Guildenstern suffered the same fate; even Hamlet's direct challenge to them, "Were you not sent for?" was omitted.

One of Salvini's oddest adjustments to the play was the removal of the players from this act. Though Polonius introduced them, they did not appear. Instead Salvini cried out "They are most welcome" with such enthusiasm and delight that it was clear his idea of how to employ them for his own ends had occurred to him at once. He then threw himself with much passion into the declamation of the lines concerning the daughter of Jephtha, so much so that Polonius's lines about the speaker turning his color and having tears in his eyes were made to refer to Hamlet in his delivery of this passage rather than to the player. Of course this completely destroyed the motivation behind the subsequent "O what a rogue and peasant slave am I" soliloquy, but this seems to have given Salvini no concern. Apparently the soliloquies gave such opportunities for display that a star could not omit one, whether it made any sense in his adaptation or not.

Salvini's second act did not end here, but continued directly into the next scene between the King, Queen, Rosencrantz, and Guildenstern, followed by "To be or not to be." Salvini's delivery of this famous soliloquy was almost universally praised. He avoided the stilted and histrionic approach then common for the speech, assuming a natural, quiet, and meditative tone, though one with great power and intelligence. Apparently only twice was the speech reinforced by gesture, once when he gave a start as if seized by a pang of terror on "perchance to dream," and again when he pointed a finger slowly and impressively downward on "the undiscovered country." This latter was considered a particularly imaginative stroke since Hamlets traditionally cast their eyes heavenward at this line instead of pointing in the direction of the grave. The only negative comments concerning the soliloquy came from those who admitted its power but felt that such philosophical musing was unsuited to the energetic and powerful Hamlet Salvini portrayed in the rest of the play. The *New York Herald* of 3 October 1873, for example, called the soliloquy "a striking effort in delivery and gesticulation, animated, descriptive, pictorial, and neat," but went on to observe that it "seemed about as relevant to the state of his mind as a brief discourse might have been on the quality of yellow turnips or the price of pork."

The scene with Ophelia was generally regarded, especially by American critics, as one of the production's most tender and beautiful sequences. Salvini departed sharply from tradition here, playing a scene usually rendered with violent and extravagant declamation with the utmost gentleness and pathetic sadness. *Century Magazine* suggested that he found the emotional center of the scene in the words "What should such fellows as I do, crawling between earth and heaven. We are arrant knaves all—believe none of us—get thy ways to a nunnery."

> The words "*Al chiostro!*" are whispered, almost sighed forth, with unexampled tenderness and compassion. By his sincerity of belief in his own unworthiness he excites our sympathy for himself scarcely less than for her.[7]

Immediately after this moment, the King and Polonius moved from their hiding place and Hamlet caught sight of them from the corner of his eye. He turned and faced Ophelia with a changed and moody brow, but still he did not indulge in the traditional violence or abuse. Instead he began speaking in a sort of childish singsong which was his indication of feigned madness, never raising his voice above a colloquial tone. For the lines which he wished to emphasize, such as "Get thee to a nunnery" and "I have heard of your paintings," he relied upon striking facial expressions (some called them grimaces) rather than changing the pitch of his voice. His madness here, as always, was clearly feigned, for it was Salvini's conviction that Hamlet was never close to actual mental unbalance. Nor did he labor, especially in this scene, to make the deception a particularly effective one, since his greater concern was with sparing Ophelia pain. Under these circumstances, her line "Oh, what a noble mind is here o'erthrown" seemed hardly appropriate and was cut. The scene (as well as the act) ended with Hamlet's "To a nunnery, go!" This, of course, had the additional advantage of giving the curtain line to Salvini.

The next act began with Claudius's next speech, "Love! His affections do not that way tend," and moved quickly, omitting the advice to the players and greatly reducing Hamlet's conversation with Horatio, to the play-within-the-play scene. In the composition of this scene, widely considered one of his best,

Salvini departed from the traditional English arrangement which put the players upstage center and Hamlet and the King downstage left and right. The players instead performed downstage right (thus causing some sight-line problems on that side of the auditorium), the King was seated across from them downstage, with Hamlet up center. Horatio's position, according to the *Saturday Review*, was both unusual and unsatisfactory:

> Horatio follows out so faithfully Hamlet's command to observe his uncle that he stands alone, far apart from the rest of the Court, and directly opposite to the King, in such a position that he cannot possibly see what passes on the mimic stage, but can and does fix his eyes most constantly upon Claudius.[8]

Salvini sat at Ophelia's feet, avoiding the traditional recumbent or semi-recumbent position, and held a manuscript presumably containing the dialogue of the play to be given. Salvini used these papers both as a screen to hide his glances at Claudius and as a device to indicate his mounting nervous excitement, giving them first a tremor, then a distinct rustle, and finally feverishly gnawing them. At "You shall see anon how the murderer gets the love of Gonzago's wife," Salvini rushed upon the King, fairly shouting the plot of the play in Claudius's face, so that the King's response seemed as much to this attack as to the play itself. As Claudius rushed from the stage, Salvini threw the papers into the air and fell into Horatio's arms with an inarticulate cry of triumph amid a shower of falling pages. This striking tableau replaced the "stricken deer" verses of the original, and was widely praised, though it was not, a number of both English and American reviewers noted, original with Salvini. The same device had been employed by Fechter, and before him by Kemble, who was said to have been the first to substitute papers for the traditional fan.

In keeping with Salvini's suppression of the light and ironic side of Hamlet, the recorder scene was cut, and also the interchange with Polonius concerning the shape of "yonder cloud." Instead, immediately after the embrace of Horatio, Rosencrantz and Guildenstern appeared for a brief interchange not in Shakespeare informing Hamlet that the Queen wished to see him. Hamlet dismissed them and launched at once into the "witching time of night" soliloquy, immediately followed, as in Shakespeare, by the scene containing the King's prayer. During the nineteenth century, this scene was traditionally played with the King's long speech before the prayer cut, but with the preceding interchange between Claudius, Rosencrantz, Guildenstern, and Polonius retained. Salvini reversed this, cutting the opening of the scene but keeping the King's speech, a choice generally praised by the reviewers. Less approved was his decision to set this scene in the Queen's chamber, from which Hamlet had to exit and then reenter. This was apparently done to solve a problem which sometimes bothers viewers of the play—that is, whether Hamlet really thinks the King, whom he left in prayer, could somehow have come to the Queen's room and hidden behind the arras so quickly.

The scene between Hamlet and Gertrude was widely regarded as the high point of Salvini's *Hamlet* and was a revelation to its audiences. Most Hamlets they had seen appeared before the Queen as calm, dispassionate mentors, reasoning gently and perhaps sorrowfully with Gertrude's better self. Salvini, in the words of the *Boston Globe*:

> turns upon her with a torrent of fierce invection; thunders in her ears the fiery denunciation of her crime, til she shrinks in abject terror into the depths of her chair and covers her ears to shut out the dreadful accusations. There is no reasoning, no expostulation. Hamlet appears to her the avenging executioner, and physical fear is added to her mental anguish.[9]

Some critics praised Salvini's passionate intensity in this scene, while others admitted its impressiveness but considered it a particularly striking example of the actor's misconception of the character of Hamlet. Irritated by these reactions, Salvini argued not only that his interpretation was true to the original, but even that it was a comparatively dispassionate one:

> I think that in *Hamlet* I adhere closely to the poet's idea in this sense—that Shakespeare wanted to make a man weak in purpose but with a great mind. Hamlet is undecided in his

resolutions. Some critics in this country have said that I am too violent in certain scenes. Hamlet's speeches to the Queen would give the idea, and it has, that the character is a violent one; but I think my treatment of the role is very subdued. I have seen Rossi, Davenport, Kean, and a number of good actors in the part, and they are far more violent than I am. I can only account for this objection from the fact that my voice is sonorous, and when I speak my voice may sound a little too loud.[10]

In the portrait sequence Salvini grew quieter and introduced another striking and much-praised innovation. Instead of referring to specific tangible miniatures in the traditional manner, he knelt down by the Queen and conjured up imaginary visions of the two Kings in the air before them. Completing the image of his departed father, he lessened the impact of the sequence, some reviewers felt, by putting his fingers together, placing them to his lips, and blowing an audible kiss to the enchanting vision, a gesture scorned by the *New York Times* as "thoroughly Latin, or we might almost say French." Turning now to the portrait of Claudius, Salvini, in the words of *Century Magazine:*

> gradually reaches his highest eloquence of delivery, expression and action. The climax of passion seems to be reached at the words, "A king of shreds and patches," but at that moment he beholds the apparition of his father, and we see that the climax had been yet to come. The sudden break in his voice as he appeals to the "heavenly guards" to save and shield him, the attitude of awe and admiration which he instantaneously assumes, combine to produce an ineffaceable and utterly indescribable effect.[11]

After giving one of his impressive backward starts, Salvini watched trembling as the phantom crossed the stage, indicating his disturbance by inarticulate movements of his lips and inexplicable—to the Queen—pointings of his hand. The ghost, instead of simply stalking across the stage in the usual manner, appeared suddenly from a trap, and then glided through the scene without apparent effort, an effect much admired and admirably suited to the line "Why, look you there! Look, how it steals away!"

Here also in his commentary Salvini stressed the abrupt change in Hamlet when confronted by the ghost. Before this moment he addresses his mother "with a passionate vehemence, for a moment, driven to exasperation by the thought of the difference between the character of his father and his uncle" but afterward, "he should be sorry for his outburst and gently appeal to her, begging her to repent."[12] To emphasize this, Salvini markedly changed his tone. His voice became thin and tremulous and he delivered his final pleas to the Queen almost in tears. The scene ended abruptly soon after. To Gertrude's "What shall I do?" Hamlet answered "Nothing, madam, but what I have told you. Go. Seek the King. Tell him all I've said and further, that my madness is not true, but feigned. Mother, farewell." Presumably neither Salvini nor his Italian translator recognized that Hamlet was giving the opposite counsel in the original; indeed, in interviews about this play Salvini usually cited the mistranslated line as evidence for his conviction that Hamlet's lunacy was totally feigned, without, unfortunately, explaining just what purpose Hamlet then had for this pretense.[13] Salvini's third act ended immediately after this line, with all references to the disposal of the body and Hamlet's subsequent conversations with the courtiers and the King omitted.

The fourth act began with Hamlet's soliloquy "How all occasions do inform against me" but, since all previous material in this scene had been cut, the opening of the soliloquy was rewritten to contain some rather awkward exposition, thus:

> How all occasions do inform against me
> And spur my dull revenge! I hear the powers
> Of Norway with Fortinbras their leader march
> Through Denmark, etc.

Signora Piamonti as Ophelia was universally praised for her mad scene, some critics going so far as to suggest that it struck the only authentically Shakespearian note in the play. Like Salvini she was highly effective in suggesting her thoughts by an attitude or an expression. One much-praised touch was when, encountering Laertes, her features were illuminated by a flash of memory and she made a motion to embrace him before the cloud of madness descended upon her again. The plotting scene between Laertes and Claudius followed immediately and was brief and passionate. The scene, and the act, ended not with the King expressing concern over Laertes's rage, but with the stirring, but non-Shakespearian interchange:

Claudius: Now grief conquers anger, but then—
Laertes: Vengeance!

The gravedigger scene opening act 5 was heavily cut, in keeping with Salvini's avoidance of comic touches. He was praised for his quiet and natural delivery of this scene, which he played seated on a neighboring stone and chatting casually with the single gravedigger. Less praise was given to the appearance of Ophelia's body on a bier instead of in a closed coffin, a touch many felt carried realism too far. The encounter with Laertes Salvini played with violent passion, made all the more striking by his quiet opening of the act. The play then moved rapidly to its conclusion. Hamlet's revelation to Horatio of the events of the sea voyage was cut, and of the Osric scene only basic exposition was kept, without a hint of the character of the gilded waterfly. Salvini's grace and skill in the climactic duel were much praised, but the exchange of rapiers gave the audience a shock. Salvini clapped his hand to his side at the moment he realized he was wounded, then continued the duel with affected indifference, disarmed Laertes and, with a meaning smile and bow, offered him his own foil in exchange. This device, instead of the text's ambiguous "in scuffling they change rapiers," has been frequently employed in modern productions, and in fact was not original with Salvini. Dumas employed it at his Théâtre Historique production in 1848. Still, it was unfamiliar to English and American audiences in the 1870s, and it provided evidence to those who interpreted Salvini's Hamlet as a cold-blooded, Italianate, vendetta-inspired figure.

Once the foils were exchanged, Salvini attacked Laertes with awesome ferocity, pushing aside all the ceremonial forms of the duel. When Laertes and Claudius had both received their death wounds only a few lines remained, since the English Ambassadors, Fortinbras, even Horatio's offer to die with Hamlet were all cut. Hamlet's final speech was that ending "Horatio, I am dead; Thou livest; report me and my cause aright to the unsatisfied." The dying prince then reached out for the head of his friend, and drew it down for a departing kiss. "No more pathetic death has ever been seen on the stage," said George Henry Lewes.[14] Horatio then delivered the play's final line: "O noble heart! He is gone!"

In 1886, when Salvini and Booth made brief appearances in Philadelphia, Boston, and Brooklyn playing Othello and Iago, Salvini played the Ghost to Booth's Hamlet once in each city. In this role he had few opportunities to utilize his pantomimic skills, but he made maximum use of the rich, resonant, and highly flexible voice which many felt was his greatest asset as an actor. The most detailed account of his interpretation appeared in the *Philadelphia Evening Bulletin*, which said, in part:

> He wore a helmet and a coat of mail, without the enveloping gauze that has commonly been employed to indicate ghostliness. He had a heavy, spreading beard, a sword hung at his side, and he carried the usual sceptre. At his back was draped a mantle. His demeanor did not have the automatic stiffness assumed by ordinary actors of the role, but in aspect and motion he was essentially vital and forceful. The same freedom from English traditions was heard when he spoke, for he did not intone the lines monotonously, but gave to them much variety of expression, his grand voice going from vehement loudness to a tremulous whisper. He was less piteous and more resentful than the Ghost to whom we are accustomed. He did not supplicate, but commanded Hamlet to avenge his murder.[15]

Salvini's power in this role was all the more striking as it was not a part normally interpreted by major actors. Not surprisingly, he was almost universally praised, though he probably gained little satisfaction from comments such as that of the 1 May 1886 *New York Tribune*, which heaped encomiums upon his interpretation and then concluded: "It is not too much to say that in this performance of the Ghost Signor Salvini gave a deeper and clearer impression of his intellectual grasp of this subject of Hamlet than he has before given by his performance of Hamlet itself."

7
Salvini's *Macbeth*

Salvini's *Macbeth* never achieved the popular success of his *Othello*, but a significant number of critics, in America if not in England, considered it his greatest Shakespearian creation. He presented the play almost uncut, thus avoiding the irritations caused by his much-adapted *Hamlet,* and he found in Macbeth a character more congenial to his powerful and physical delivery than the contemplative prince. In his own opinion Macbeth was a kind of antithesis of Hamlet. "If the play of *Hamlet* expresses the force of thought over action," he said, "that of *Macbeth* may be considered as illustrating the predominance of action over thought."[1] In an interview in Chicago he spoke of the character in terms which suggested a strong affinity with his popular Othello:

> Before he commits his first crime he is a warrior, proud, bold, and daring. . . . All through the play, even after the commission of the first crime, he retains his pride; and when he is besieged on every side with difficulties he feels like a lion in a den struck at by people he cannot reach.[2]

The first appearance of Macbeth, like that of Othello, was dazzling—a colossal figure in full fighting gear and a flowing cape, with long tawny hair and a thick beard, made more colossal still by a spiked helmet with towering wings. All of Salvini's costumes for this production were designed by Gustave Doré, who did research in Scotland to discover the most impressive as well as the most authentic dress possible.

Salvini's interpretation of the opening scenes was generally conventional, given the powerful, relaxed, and self-assured nature of his Macbeth. He started almost instinctively when the weird sisters hailed him as future king, and he indicated clearly his displeasure and distress when Duncan seemed to thwart this promise by naming Malcolm as his heir, but otherwise his self-possession never wavered. A distinctly individual note began to be struck in the first scene with Lady Macbeth, a scene marked by an easy and colloquial tone much different from the intense and ominous reading traditionally given to it. Henry James found this a quality of the entire production. Despite its great variety, it deserved "the great praise of being temperate and discreet;" indeed "much of it is very quiet," and there was not a touch of the rant or violence so common to productions James had seen.[3] Lady Macbeth was often interpreted as the instigating agent in this scene (especially of course when an actress like Ristori was playing the role), but Salvini's Macbeth was clearly his own master. The insinuating words of his wife merely corroborated a decision he had already reached. The only outside persuasion to which he was subject was apparently that of the weird sisters. In reply to Lady Macbeth's "And when goes hence?" Salvini paused a moment, looked furtively about, and replied "Tomorrow, as *he* proposes." When Lady Macbeth responded "O, never shall sun that morrow see!" his face lighted up to find her so apt a reader of his own thoughts.

In the soliloquy "If it were done when 'tis done," Salvini began to show the effects of waiting and of contemplation on this man of action. He stood, the very picture of "letting I dare not wait upon I would," passing his hands through his leonine hair, stroking his beard, pulling it impatiently, fumbling at his sword belt in the bitterest doubt and hesitation until his wife appeared, to reconfirm him in his resolution. He still hesitated until her line "But screw your courage to the sticking-place, and we'll not fail." Then, as she suggested the details of the assassination, he began to look up, open-mouthed, his moody brow clearing, his formerly downcast eyes gazing on her with mixed astonishment and admiration. When she finished, he embraced her with delight, a striking and unconventional gesture which Robert Louis Stevenson felt contained the key to their relationship:

> The nature of his feeling toward her is rendered with a most precise and delicate touch. He always yields to the woman's fascination; and yet his caresses (and we know how much meaning Salvini can give to a caress) are singularly hard and unloving. Sometimes he lays his hand on her as he might take hold of any one who happened to be nearest him at a moment of excitement. Love has fallen out of this marriage by the way, and left a curious friendship. Only once—at the very moment when she is showing herself so little a woman and so much a high-spirited man—only once is he very deeply stirred towards her; and that finds expression in the strange and horrible transport of admiration, doubly strange and horrible on Salvini's lips—"Bring forth men-children only."[4]

The great soliloquy of the second act, "Is this a dagger which I see before me," drew conflicting responses from the critics, depending on whether they were impressed or irritated by Salvini's untraditional delivery. As was his custom with soliloquies, he presented it for the most part in a quiet, conversational tone, devoid of rhetorical flourish, only occasionally giving particular emphasis to a word or passage either by a more intense tone or by illustrative gesture. As a result the soliloquy became not a set piece, but a series of isolated effects. Audiences were clearly aware of this, and tended to interrupt the passage with bursts of applause instead of giving a single ovation at the end as they normally did with more traditional readings. Naturally there were also complaints that such individual effects distracted from the soliloquy as a whole, especially when they were deemed overly illustrative. On the line "Mine eyes are made the fools o' the other senses," the critic of the *Saturday Review* complained that "with a view to emphasizing the line, when he speaks of his eyes, he rubs them. How ludicrously prosaic this appears need not be said."[5]

Macbeth's costume in this act was one of several which also

aroused complaints, despite its presumed authenticity. It was of a bright green corded silk, trimmed with fur and with sleeves of so vivid a hue that the blood which covered his hands seemed to extend to his shoulders. Still, this somewhat bizarre dress was soon forgotten in the power of Salvini's acting after the murder. He rushed from Duncan's chamber in horror, so frenzied by fear and superstitious dread that he did not at first recognize his wife. He jostled against her, uttered an inarticulate cry, and raised his dagger to strike before he came to his senses. His "Here's a sorry sight" was groaned out with accents of the most heartfelt agony, and he continued his story in broken phrases as his wife attempted in vain to soothe him with soft words and caresses. The *Saturday Review* critic who had found the interpretation of the dagger soliloquy so offensive found the reading of " 'Amen' stuck in my throat," "worse still, if possible. . . . Here he absolutely rehearses to his wife the futile efforts he made to pronounce the 'Amen.' "[6] The majority of audience and reviewers, however, found this passage extremely effective. In the words of the *New York World:*

> Nothing could exceed the piteousness of his accents when he murmured brokenly that one of the guards had said "Amen," and that he could not say Amen. It was most thrilling. It expressed mental anguish as perhaps none of the audience had heard it before, and it confirmed and strengthened the conception of Macbeth's superstition and his mental inferiority to his wife.[7]

At the end of the scene Salvini invariably received one of his largest ovations of the evening, and the minority of critics who had felt the sequence overdone and unconvincing were treated to the further irritation of seeing Salvini, after staggering up the steps to the door of his chamber to wash off the blood, return to the footlights to bow in acknowledgement of the plaudits.

In the sequence immediately after this, Salvini followed Shakespeare much more closely than most of his contemporaries. He restored the almost universally cut porter, and returned quiet and unarmed to bid Macduff welcome and to let him discover the body instead of omitting all this, as did some other Macbeths of the period, in order to greet the stunned arriving party with a frenzied air, a bloody sword, and the news that the murder has just been discovered and the grooms killed.

John Coleman, who had little good to say about the Doré costumes anywhere in the production, found Macbeth's in the third act particularly offensive.

> The usurper's regal robes were of white silver lamé, the material affected by fairies and burlesque princes in the pantomimes. A delicately-jewelled filigree waistbelt vainly attempted to restrain the rebellious region which obstinately persisted in asserting itself.[8]

This rich display did, however, make a striking contrast with the ragged murderers, especially when at the close of the scene one of them in fawning obeisance attempted to seize and kiss the hem of Macbeth's robe. Salvini's reaction combined imperial disdain with a shudder of loathing as he pulled away the garment—a moment considered extremely effective.

Other effective innovations appeared in the following murder scene itself. Salvini restored the third murderer, traditionally omitted, and showed Banquo being cut down by the daggers of the assassins instead of placing his murder offstage. The banquet scene was generally considered the high point of this production. The *New York Times* said Salvini played it with "an affluence of art which was unmarred by the faintest false effect," and the *Boston Globe* called it "a marvel of intensity," continuing:

> The adjuration to the spirit to be gone, with the frenzy of motion and gesture, with horror and despair voiced in his words and depicted on his face, thrilled even the most blasé of theatre-goers. Here the actor towered above all who have essayed the part; here Salvini was Macbeth himself.[9]

The triumph of the scene was Salvini's alone, for the visual accompaniment he received drew kind words from no one. Doré may have attempted, in his idiosyncratic way, to create costumes for the star with a certain historical authenticity, but no such care went into the dress of the rest of the company or into the setting. French chandeliers and fine linen tablecloths contrasted oddly with rude furnishings and antique goblets. John Coleman mentions a whole series of similar oddities:

> The music selected for the opening of the banquet was a Scotch jig, usually associated with the Highland fling. The half-empty stage was sparsely populated by pale, squalid guests, attired in tawdry costumes of all periods and all nations. These poor creatures gazed helplessly and hopelessly at the tinfoil trumpery before them, while they ate not, drank not, neither did they make merry. The ghost of Banquo, in the first instance, scrambled up from under a table, tumbled down again, and re-appeared from a front-trap, jerked up like a Harlequin.[10]

Coleman also found grotesque Salvini's exit from the scene after the departure of the guests, though there were critics who praised it as a masterstroke. As Lady Macbeth started off stage she let fall her white veil, and the terrified Macbeth, thinking for an instant that the phantom had reappeared, first recoiled in horror, and then, unsheathing his dagger, rushed upon the veil as if to murder it again, thrusting at it as the curtain fell upon the act.

The chief scene of Salvini's fourth act was the encounter with Hecate and the witches in which Macbeth receives their final prophecies. Macbeth's delight in the seemingly favorable predictions, and his surprise, rage, and desperation as the descendants of Banquo began to appear were portrayed by Salvini with his usual effectiveness, and a striking piece of business closed the scene. When the shadow of Banquo appeared at the end of the procession, Salvini sprang forward, sword in hand, as if to attack this vision. Then he suddenly paused, realizing its insubstantial nature, and with a groan fell senseless to the earth. The witches then danced over him with mysterious and grotesque posturings, upon which the act-drop descended.

Salvini was moderately fortunate in his Lady Macbeths—Signora Piamonti in England and Marie Prescott in America both provided stronger support for him than was usual for touring stars. As a result the sleepwalking scene was generally considered highly moving and effective, though never of course rivalling that of Ristori. Probably Salvini himself gave particular attention to this scene, for in his comments on the play he makes the surprising suggestion that Shakespeare must surely have meant this scene originally for Macbeth, since it reveals a remorse and weakness in Lady Macbeth not elsewhere suggested. "Had the play been written in our time," Salvini concludes, "the presumption would be that the change was made at the caprice of some charming actress who did not find the part assigned to her sufficiently important."[11]

The Macduffs were not only mediocre actors, but no match for Salvini physically, so that the final duel, carried out with swords and daggers, lost much of its possible power. The rest of the final battle was less impressive still. Malcolm's army consisted only of a dozen lank and slender-limbed soldiers, whose appearance with large green boughs held in front of them was distinctly more comic than imposing. At the line "your heavy screens throw down, and show like those you are," they obediently dropped the boughs in a mathematically straight line in front of the footlights and marched off into the wings, whereupon a group of stagehands appeared to gather up the greenery so that the play could continue. In the following battle, according to Coleman:

> Some twenty or thirty wretched supernumeraries in nondescript costumes came scrambling over the stage, in a kind of bungled mêlée, during which they exchanged an occasional crack on the head, or tumbled over one another, as the spirit moved them, with charming impartiality.[12]

In short, except for the sleepwalking scene, Salvini was forced to provide the final act with whatever dramatic power it was to possess on his own and, though he achieved a modest success in this, the act boasted no scenes nor moments comparable to the best sequences in earlier acts. Robert Louis Stevenson stood almost alone in calling this act Salvini's best, and Stevenson was considering no particular sequence but the way in which Salvini had modulated from the proud and self-satisfied hero of the beginning to the haunted, decadent tyrant of the end:

> This is still the big, burly, fleshly, handsome looking Thane; here is still the same face which in the earlier acts could be superficially good-humoured and sometimes royally courteous. But now the atmosphere of blood, which pervades the whole tragedy, has entered into the man and subdued him to its own nature; and an indescribable degradation, a slackness and puffiness, has overtaken his features.[13]

A barely contained fury and disgust lay beneath every action of Macbeth now. The news of the death of his wife staggered him, and he fell into a chair and covered his face briefly with his hands; but the subsequent line "Tomorrow, and tomorrow, and tomorrow" showed little affliction, rather a tragic cynicism which was much admired. In the fight with Macduff, all the initiative lay with Macbeth, and the advantage was all his until the fatal discovery that his opponent was not "of woman born." The look of amazement, then of mortal terror which passed over his features showed the audience plainly that the end had come, and in the brief remainder of the fight he made so poor a defense that it appeared almost a suicide. Since Macbeth was provided with no dying speech and the final curtain had to fall as quickly as possible after the death of the star, the ending of *Macbeth*, immediately after this final duel, was the most abrupt and truncated of any of Salvini's Shakespearian offerings.

8
Salvini's *King Lear*

King Lear was longer in preparation than any of Salvini's other Shakespearian roles; he studied it for five years before presenting it to the public in 1882. His basic problem in coming to terms with the play was a familiar one to any would-be interpreter of this titanic role: the problem of striking a balance between the great age and weakness suggested in some scenes and the massive force and power demanded by others. "I could bend my form and so far assume the part of an old decrepit man," said Salvini, "but once fired with the enthusiasm which seems necessary to make the play real to the actor, I found it hard, indeed impossible, to restrain my energy and make my countenance, my voice, and my action fall to the lower key needful to properly delineate the actual Lear, or as he should be in the final acts."[1]

Not long after his creation of *Macbeth*, Salvini was indeed reported to have given up solving this dilemma by technical means alone and was said to be simply awaiting the time, "which he does not consider far distant, when the fatigues and excitements of his career will have sufficiently broken his robust technique to enable him to enact the part of Lear."[2] This report has the feel of a publicity ploy about it; and in any case, Salvini was certainly not in declining health when in 1882 he finally undertook this demanding role. He now significantly no longer spoke of an "old decrepit man" but instead of a "centenarian oak from which the violence of the winds and the fury of the storm may pluck the leaves, but whose stems and trunk remain vigorous and tenacious."[3] He was now, said Henry James, at the age when he could "lawfully approach" the part, yet when "his extraordinary bodily and vocal powers give definite assurance of sustaining him."[4] Less enthusiastic critics complained that his Lear was too healthy and well-preserved, or at least that he was so vigorous in key scenes that his scenes of physical weakness were not entirely convincing.

Salvini's entrance suggested a certain infirmity; he moved with a slow, heavy step, the step of a large, portly, and very old man, but one still possessed of considerable strength. He haughtily brushed aside the offer of a courtier to help him to his throne, raised on a slight dais, and seated himself, a still majestic leonine figure with a profuse iron-gray wig and beard. The formality of his court was somewhat diminished by his unusual placement of Lear behind a large conference table, upon which the map was unrolled. Salvini said that in this act Lear "remains ever the majestic irascible tyrant," and in the opening scene there was no hint of senility or indecisiveness, although the rage of the thwarted autocrat came readily to the surface. He described the partition of the kingdom in cool, considered tones, as if any contradiction of his will were unthinkable. He received the fulsome speeches of Goneril and Regan with a chuckle of satisfaction. Only when Cordelia spoke did the facade of the benign despot dissolve. For a moment his rage burst forth and Salvini even rushed upon the faithful Kent with drawn sword, but his stability was soon as strikingly restored. William Winter describes the sequence:

> The sensible words of Cordelia appeared to daze him with amazement. He spoke with harsh deliberation, in disclaiming her, became convulsed with hysterical fury at Kent's attempt to expostulate, and then, curbing himself, and standing silent for almost a minute (which is a long time on the stage), delivered the edict of banishment of that nobleman in a perfectly self-controlled, judicial manner.[5]

The second scene, introducing the Gloucester subplot, was presented essentially intact, the major cut being Edmund's speech, "This is the excellent foppery of the world." The jokes of the fool in the fourth scene were heavily cut, but Salvini's major change was in the ending of this scene, which built to and culminated in Lear's curse on Goneril. Here Salvini turned the full force of his outraged dignity on his daughter, striding about the stage in a fury. Henry James found a "touch of the sublime" and "an invention quite in his grandest manner" in the "wild mixture of familiarity and solemnity" with which Salvini began this passage,[6] and Salvini intensified the emotional power of the moment by means of a sudden pause and abrupt shift in tone halfway through the speech. The *New York Herald* of 9 February 1883 thus described the effect:

> Salvini excelled in the vehement scenes, and yet his violence was so well within his control that when, in the midst of cursing his daughter, he made his appeal to nature, he stood calm, irradiated, as though the heavens had suddenly opened and shed their peace upon him.

A moment later Salvini was again in passionate wrath, mounting to the line "How sharper than a serpent's tooth it is to have a thankless child." He then transfixed his daughter with a withering glance (as the audience, according to the *Philadelphia Public Ledger,* rose cheering), then wheeled about and strode from the stage as the act curtain fell. The only problem with so effective a moment was that it made Lear still seem totally master of the situation, an impression which Salvini maintained in his later confrontations with his rebellious daughters.

In the second act, Salvini felt, Lear should be represented more as a father than as a king, and he should be shown gradually becoming aware of the full extent of his daughters' ingratitude.[7] No reviewer suggests, however, that this resulted in any softening of tone—his was still the voice and attitude of majesty and command throughout the act. Only as the act was drawing toward its close did Salvini begin to indicate his pain and sorrow, and this long-awaited reaction proved enormously powerful. "I gave you all—" says William Winter, was an exquisite point, and Lear's "No, I'll not weep," which concluded the act, was felt by many to be the grandest and most moving moment in the production. Emma Lazarus wrote:

> Was there ever before concentrated in a human voice such desperate anguish of suppressed sobs, such utter fruitlessness of revolt against unnatural cruelty, as Salvini expresses in these words? He is broken, helpless, and defeated—not with the helplessness of a violent, doting old man, but with the despair of a Titan at war with demons.[8]

The act ended immediately after this powerful speech, and the following scene between Cornwall, Regan, Gloucester, and Goneril preparing for the storm scenes on the heath was omitted. This was the most significant cut in the second act, though some of Edmund's lines were gone and the sallies of the fool were again much reduced.

The storm scene was generally considered a disappointment. The setting which accompanied Salvini for most of his performances was ludicrously inappropriate—a verdant German landscape with fleecy clouds floating in an azure sky, and a jumble of painted rocks which served only to interfere with the audience's view of the actor. The special effects were equally unimpressive; a small spattering noise came from the wings in one corner of the stage to suggest rain, and for the thunder a bass drum was struck at the rear of the stage, sometimes before and sometimes after the lightning. Salvini had little control over these physical surroundings, which were provided by the tour manager, but he may have wished to keep the noise of the storm to a minimum, for his Lear in this scene was played in a surprisingly low key. Apparently he felt that too strong a presentation here, at a traditional point of strong vocal and physical delivery, would contradict the gradual enfeeblement of Lear which he was attempting to suggest. Said William Winter:

> In delivering the first speech in the Storm, "Blow, winds, and crack your cheeks," etc., Salvini walked slowly down a set "run-way," from the right of the stage, so that his figure was half-obscured by painted semblances of rocks, and he *grumbled* the speech, all the way, in a low, monotonous voice, producing no effect whatever, except of tedious ineptitude.[9]

Salvini's quiet and more tender moments in this scene were far more successful, and his interpretation of the line beginning "My wits begin to turn" inspired much praise. As he said "Come on, my boy: how dost, my boy? art cold?" he turned from his own sufferings, with the warmest affection, to protect the fool, and with the greatest grace and dignity removed his own mantle to wrap it about the fool's shivering shoulders. Then, feeling the bitter blast in his turn ("I am cold myself"), he wrapped the fool in a paternal embrace, seeking shelter under the same enveloping cloak, and escorted him from the stage to conclude the scene. Here could be most clearly seen the working out of Salvini's idea that in the third act Lear's physical sufferings pushed aside his moral ones, as the king gave way to the tormented human being.[10] At this point, though Salvini had made Lear's suffering clear enough, he had still not suggested a touch of madness. This did not really appear until the second scene with the disguised Edgar (William Winter says the first clear indication came with the line "To have a thousand with red burning spits"). Now Lear became more erratic, more extreme in movement, gesture, and vocal inflection. The space about him became filled with imaginary beings which drew his eyes and his attention. On "Now, you she foxes!" he seemed to see them running away from his anger, and pursued them full tilt as far as the footlights. This approach was used throughout the mock trial which, since Salvini omitted the scene containing the blinding of Gloucester, was the final scene of the third act. The act's closing line was Lear's "We'll go to supper i' the morning," so the fool was deprived of his last speech in the play, "And I'll go to bed at noon."

The first two scenes of the fourth act (both somewhat cut) were presented in reversed order. Thus the act began with news of the landed army of invasion and Albany's discovery of the blinding of Gloucester. This latter thus served as exposition for the ensuing scene 1 of act 4, showing the blinded father's first encounter with Edgar. Scenes 3, 4, and 5 were cut, so that this Edgar-Gloucester scene led directly into the mock climbing of the hill near Dover. Lear's entrance, crowned with flowers, Salvini played quietly and pathetically, preparing for the most striking effect in the play, another of those sudden and unexpected surges of Lear's former power. When Gloucester asked "Is't not the King?" Salvini stared at him for a moment, as if marshalling his wandering wits to deal with the question. Then, suddenly comprehending, he rushed up a mound the elevation of which exactly corresponded to the dais of his former throne, tore a branch from a tree placed there, and holding it as a sceptre, thundered majestically "Ay, every inch a King!"—an effect inevitably inspiring applause and cheers. Similarly, though less strikingly, the effect of the contrast between the gentle and pathetic "It were a delicate stratagem, to shoe a troop of horse with felt" and the rage of the six times repeated "kill!" was much admired. After Lear's exit from this scene, a single short speech by Gloucester:

> You ever-gentle gods, take my breath from me;
> Let not my worser spirit tempt me again
> To die before you please!

served as the bridge to the entrance of Oswald. The scene was then played uncut to its conclusion.

In the final scene of the fourth act Salvini reached the section of the play which put his interpretation to the greatest test. Seeing Lear as "robust and strong in the beginning, distressed and agitated next, enfeebled and touching in the end," he admitted that this placed the greatest difficulty in the closing scenes, where he sought "through physical weakness to reveal once more the last flickering of an expiring torch."[11] This created a dynamic directly opposed to that normally expected by audiences of a star production, and indeed normally utilized by Salvini himself, as the critic of *Temple Bar* noted:

This study of the King's strength and feebleness was a deep one with Salvini. He knew very well that in order to raise the interest of the public more and more, gradually increasing effects are the most efficacious means; and it would have been easy to save his *"sortie,"* i.e. his last act, by such a *crescendo,* if I may so call it. Salvini knew it, but he sacrificed his effect to the invariable law of his life, artistic truth.[12]

In so doing, Salvini was of course taking a risk, but if he could gain his effect, the unusual means of doing so would themselves vastly increase its power. Artistic truth was doubt-less important in this choice, but Salvini was certainly percep-tive enough to realize that in sacrificing the conventional effect, he created an opportunity to achieve a more striking and unex-pected one. The degree of his success may be suggested by the comments of the critic of the *Chicago Tribune,* who noted that the recognition scene was played "in a key subdued, perhaps be-yond all precedent," and continued:

> Not a trace of autocratic dignity remains; there is no surging of the passion for justice, for revenge; only a joy, so far be-yond language that it strikes upon the heart like pain. Here Signor Salvini gave proof of a power which one had not suspected in him—that of producing the greatest effect of the play without the help of physical impressiveness. . . . When the old man sank at his daughter's feet for pardon the action smote upon the heart-strings of the audience even as it must have done upon the surprised soul of Cordelia. To one who has admired Signor Salvini in moments of physical force the pathos that he breathed through absolute weakness was a revelation.[13]

Salvini's fifth act began with Edmund's speech "To both these sisters have I sworn my love," followed by the inter-change between Edgar and Albany which immediately pre-cedes this speech in the original. The rest of the first scene and all of the second was cut. The third scene was then given with only minor omissions until the conclusion. Quiet pathos domi-nated this final scene in Salvini's interpretation, though there was a final touch of the old King as well as of the child in "Come, let's away to prison." The final sequence, with the dead Cordelia, was played, said Henry James, "in a muffled key,—the tone of an old man whose fire and fury have spent themselves, and who has nothing left but weakness, tears, and death." Salvini's "Howl, howl, howl," James felt, did not have "the classic resonance; but the pathos of the whole thing is unspeakable."[14]

Salvini's unusual entrance provided an effective illustration of Lear's weakness, and also of the smoldering remains of his pride. He did not carry Cordelia in his arms, but dragged her with great difficulty and effort. Then, when the others moved to aid him, he waved them back, as he had waved back the presumptuous courtier who wished at the opening of the play to help him to his throne. Whatever the difficulty, only he could touch the beloved body. Then he became entirely the grieving father. A final spark flared up on "This feather stirs! she lives!" Salvini looked wildly about, then snatched the helmet plume from Edgar's hand to place it at Cordelia's lips. When this last illusion passed, his face grew gray, his grizzled head drooped, and whispering "Look there, look there!" he fell, face downward, over Cordelia's body. Only two short lines remained before the final curtain:

Edgar: He faints! My lord, my lord!
Kent: Vex not his ghost; O, let him pass!

1. Ristori as Lady Macbeth (Folger Shakespeare Library)

2. Salvini as Othello (Folger Shakespeare Library)

3. Salvini as Hamlet (archivio fot. del Burcado)

4. Salvini as Macbeth (Harvard Theatre Collection)

5. Salvini as King Lear (Folger Shakespeare Library)

6. Salvini as Coriolanus (*Farm and Country,* Indiana University Library)

7. Rossi as Hamlet (archivio fot. del Burcado)

8. Rossi as King Lear (archivio fot. del Burcado)

9. **Rossi as King Lear (archivio fot. del Burcado)**

10. Rossi as Othello (archivio fot. del Burcado)

11. Rossi as Romeo (archivio fot. del Burcado)

12. Rossi as Macbeth (archivio fot. del Burcado)

13. Rossi as Macbeth (archivio fot. del Burcado)

9

Salvini's *Coriolanus*

In a *New York Times* interview given when Salvini was preparing to premiere his *Coriolanus*, the actor stressed his particular fitness for this role:

> I can hardly believe that Shakespeare didn't know me when he wrote it. The character suits me admirably, and it always seems to me that had I lived in those days I should, under the circumstances, have acted exactly as did Coriolanus. The man is an Italian, strong, proud, and a—a little pretentious. We all are, you know.[1]

Whether audiences were convinced of the truth of this depended as usual on whether they were willing to accept an interpretation which differed sharply from English tradition and differed in a way typical of Salvini. His Caius Marcius was an imposing, heavily bearded warrior, like his Macbeth, restless and impetuous rather than statuesque, natural and human in his reactions rather than classical and conventional. Other interpreters of the role, such as Forrest, had not been lacking in passion, but it was the proud and aloof passion of the aristocrat. Salvini, in the words of the *Chicago Tribune* of 17 January 1886, "was grandly the man, but not grandly the patrician. Indeed, he might well be regarded as a proud plebian, for all the distinction of caste that was marked in his acting."

Aside from the naturalness and finish of Salvini's creation—traits remarked in all of his Shakespearian roles—the feature of his Coriolanus which drew the most praise was its cumulative force. In this role he could develop the natural build which he felt the character of Lear denied him, beginning quietly and moving steadily upward to the emotional peaks of the performance, in a manner similar to his *Othello* and *Macbeth*. The opening scene, containing Caius Marcius's confrontation with the hungry citizens, had none of the passion and bombast common in English interpretations. Salvini's tone was moderate, touched with an almost playful sarcasm. Even the apostrophe to the prowess of Tullus Aufidius, "He is a lion that I am proud to hunt," was delivered not as a shout of challenge but as a quiet, thoughtful expression of admiration for a brave foe. His final taunt, "take these rats hither," as he turned away, was almost a private joke, delivered with a secret, scornful smile.

The second scene, in the senate house at Corioli, was not presented by Salvini, and the battle scenes of the first act were much reduced. The scenes containing the actual single-handed attack of Marcius upon the city (4 and 5) were omitted, leaving only the reports of this action in scene 6. The seventh scene was also cut, but the climactic confrontation between Marcius and Aufidius in scene 8 was retained. Given the quality of his supporting companies, from which the battle sequences in *Macbeth* suffered so severely, Salvini was doubtless wise to reduce these sequences to a minimum in *Coriolanus*. Even so, the *New York Times* of 12 November 1885 observed that "Salvini is a mighty warrior, and his combat with half a dozen Volsces would be most impressive if the Volsces themselves had fewer of the traits of the Irish-American supernumerary." The *Philadelphia Evening Bulletin* of 18 December 1885 was even more severe on the supernumeraries: "Their movements were uncertain and queer, and they marred the effort of a number of scenes, particularly those in which the action of battle or assault was to be represented."

The final two scenes of the first act were reversed so that the act could end with a star scene, and in the playing of this final scene Salvini, though unorthodox, was much praised. "The splendid passage at the close of Act I in which the sensitive modesty of the hero's nature is revealed, was acted with exquisite art," said the *New York Times*.

> There is a passage here which it has pleased Shakespearian commentators to point to as exhibiting Marcius's utter lack of sympathy with the common people. The hero has but one reward to ask for, namely, freedom for that poor citizen of Corioli who once "used him well;" but he cannot remember the citizen's name. Salvini makes it clear that the loss of memory, according to his conception, was largely due to fatigue and the chafing of his wounds. He asks for the favor in a tender, compassionate tone, but when the name is demanded, he staggers, grasps the arm of Cominius, and smiles as he presses his hand to his brow and shakes his head. The hero needs rest, for the day has been a hard one. "Have we no wine here?" he feebly asks. Surely this is a remarkable rendering of the passage. Coriolanus was proud and vindictive, but he was not heartless.[2]

The moment was clearly an effective one, but it grew organically from Salvini's emphasis on the human side of Shakespeare's hero. The *Boston Evening Transcript* of 4 December 1885 acknowledged this by remarking that, in contrast, "Forrest's Coriolanus would have died before he would have shown a sign of physical weakness."

The second act was presented almost intact. Salvini's gentle and informal delivery was particularly effective when it could be set in contrast to the background of the triumphal procession as he greeted his wife and mother. The salutation to Valeria was omitted. In the scene with the citizens in the Forum, Salvini returned to his approach of the opening sequence. There was little anger in his responses, but much contempt; no burst of passion, rather shrugs and sneers. "There is a sense of subdued emotion that is actually appalling," said the *New York World* of 12 November 1885. "The spectator comes to hope in vain for the breaking of the storm. There is an uncanny sensation of thunder—thunder without noise."

The third act gave Salvini an excellent opportunity to display rapidly shifting emotion. His long-withheld anger burst forth at the tribunes, then melted away under the reproachful words of Volumnia. This was followed by cold contempt and scorn in the scene of banishment, considered by most critics as one of the high points of the production. The *Washington Post* of 8 January 1886 called this the evening's best scene and noted that "the abusive, defiant speech was delivered with a wonderful and variously effective elocution," while the *New York Times* of 12 November 1885 said this "thrilling close" showed a "genuine power which no other actor of the present day could approach." According to the *Philadelphia Evening Bulletin*:

> Coriolanus was here grand and majestic. He dwarfed his surroundings—the malediction upon the tribunes and citizens was delivered with a passionate energy, a defiant attitude and a trumpet-toned voice. . . . It was not an outburst of pride; it was the sweeping denial and return denunciation of a man insulted.[3]

Even the plebeian supernumeraries apparently contributed something to the effect. At least the *Boston Globe* felt that there had been:

> a praiseworthy effort—more or less successful—to make the general effect of the forum scenes "realistic." The throng of plebians shouted with fervor at frequent intervals, and was threatening or enthusiastic, as the case might demand, in decidedly unanimous fashion.[4]

The act ended at the conclusion of Coriolanus's great speech, "There is a world elsewhere."

Salvini's most striking scene in the fourth act was the first, when Coriolanus parts from his family. The warmth and tenderness of these family scenes provided the actor with an excellent counterpoint to the cold scornfulness of the public appearances, thus deepening the effect of both. No other passage in this act occasioned particular remark; and indeed Salvini much reduced the act to speed on to the concluding scenes. The third and fourth scenes were omitted entirely, along with almost half of the fifth (everything after Aufidius bids welcome to Coriolanus). The act ended, uncharacteristically, not with

Coriolanus, but with the panic of the citizens at the news of his impending return in the sixth scene.

The final act began with the last scene of the traditional act 4, the conversation between Aufidius and his lieutenant concerning Coriolanus's power over the Romans, but omitting most of Aufidius's final speech on the character of his rival (everything after "I think he'll be to Rome as is the osprey to the fish"). The first two scenes of the fifth act were cut, containing the futile appeals to Coriolanus from his old friends Cominius and Menenius. Thus the climactic appeal from Volumnia stood alone in this production. Salvini's bearing during this critical scene deserved "to be studied by young actors," suggested the *New York Times* of 12 November 1885. "The value of repose was never more strikingly illustrated." In fact this repose was anything but tranquil, as the description of the sequence in the *Boston Evening Transcript* makes clear:

> His silence during her long plea was eloquence itself, for though his back was turned on her one could see in his face and in the heaving of his chest that a mighty struggle was going on within between pride and outraged honor and filial love. And what a world of meaning there was in his heart-broken cry, "O Madre!" and in his outstretched arms as Volumnia turns to go![5]

The final taunts of Aufidius, to which Coriolanus might have responded in wrath, Salvini instead received with a haughty contempt, recalling his bearing in the forum and suggesting that the great warrior knew the end was at hand and whether it came in Corioli or in Rome was immaterial to him. "Whether he spoke to friend or foe," said the *Boston Globe* of 4 December 1885, "his words were given with a simple directness and an absence of effort that showed how carefully Salvini had studied to make the role natural."

The final image of Salvini's Coriolanus thus developed directly and harmoniously from the first, steadily growing in strength as he withstood the ever-increasing external pressures brought to bear upon him. Though the role was not a particularly popular one, its artistic unity and power gained it significant critical praise. William Winter summarized Salvini's creation thus:

> He had authority, repose, and cumulative force; it is always a comfort to see an actor who can sustain and execute a splendid design, consistently, from beginning to end. That Salvini could do and that, in this case, he did.[6]

10
The Tours of Ernesto Rossi

Although Rossi accompanied Ristori to Paris in 1855 and 1856 and received favorable notice from the critics there, he was at that time quite overshadowed by his co-star. A decade passed before he returned to France with his own company to make his own bid for fame as an international star. In the intervening years he had presented *Hamlet, Othello, Romeo and Juliet, Macbeth, King Lear, The Merchant of Venice,* and *Coriolanus* in Italy, where audiences, still inclined toward traditional classic drama, accepted this experimentation with interest but without particular enthusiasm. Rossi hoped to establish a state-supported theatre in Milan, which would have given his young company a permanent home (an almost unheard-of luxury for an Italian troupe at this time), but there was insufficient support and he resigned himself to a career of continual touring. In 1865, just before his trip to Paris, he appeared with Ristori and Salvini in Florence for the Dante Festival, which was one of the great dramatic events of the period and which reconfirmed these three stars as the leaders of their generation in Italy.

His reception in Paris was far more favorable than Salvini's had been, though he had a number of advantages. Salvini had come immediately after Ristori, and probably suffered somewhat from a reaction to the extreme enthusiasm she had aroused. When Rossi came, nine years had passed since Salvini's visit, ten since his own and Ristori's, and he doubtless profited from the nostalgic memory French theatre-goers retained of the dashing young man who had supported Ristori at the time of her triumph. It was an opportune time for his arrival both politically and artistically—politically because Piedmont and France had just become allies against the Austrians, artistically because the French stage was at this moment without any major serious actors to provide Rossi with competition. His promoters called discreet attention to this fact by billing him as the "Italian Talma." Finally, he did not take the risk Salvini had of beginning with a French classic, but rather opened with *Hamlet,* followed by *Othello,* both still somewhat exotic in France but—thanks to the efforts of the romantics—perfectly acceptable.

Subsequently Rossi, like Salvini, performed in Italy only occasionally, between foreign tours. By 1874 he had appeared not only in France, but in Spain, Austria, Hungary, Germany, and South America. Then Maurice Grau, who had just sponsored Salvini's first American tour, invited Rossi to follow him. The contract was signed and preliminary bookings made, but then Rossi withdrew, forfeiting a heavy penalty, on the grounds that his son had become ill and that he did not wish to leave Europe at this time. He remained instead in Paris, for a highly successful six-month season there.

Before Rossi left Paris he received another invitation to perform Shakespeare before English-speaking audiences. Once again the success of Salvini, this time in London, encouraged entrepreneurs to consider inviting other Italian stars, and Rossi was the almost inevitable next choice. As early as 1866 his success in Paris in *Hamlet* and *Othello* had been noted by English correspondents. Mary Crowden Clarke, whose letter to the *Athenaeum* in 1864 had been one of the first reports to reach the English public about Salvini, wrote from Genoa in May of 1873 to hail Rossi's Hamlet as a creation comparable to Salvini's Othello and Ristori's Lady Macbeth.[1] At this time Salvini was still known in London only by reputation, though Ristori, after an absence of fifteen years, was about to return to perform the sleepwalking scene for the first time in English. During the following year, notices on both Rossi and Salvini appeared from time to time in the London journals, and in the spring of

1875, when Salvini at last came to perform *Othello* and *Hamlet* at Drury Lane, a report spread that Rossi would appear that same season at the Gaiety. On May 22 the *Athenæum* reported, correctly, that Rossi had in fact been engaged by Chatterton for the next season at Drury Lane.[2]

Since Salvini was also scheduled to return to London in 1876, new rumors spread, this time that the two great Italian stars might be planning to appear together, perhaps as Othello and Iago. Neither the repertoire nor the practice of either star made this speculation likely in the least, though London audiences could reasonably have expected to be given the unique opportunity to compare simultaneous productions of such plays as *Othello* and *Hamlet* by outstanding rival foreign artists. Even this opportunity, in the event, was denied them. Salvini abruptly departed after only two weeks and having offered only *Othello*, which Rossi, perhaps fearing comparison in the role acknowledged as Salvini's greatest, did not present.

Rossi remained in London for two months. He opened with *Hamlet*, his most popular role, on April 19, but was suffering from illness at the time and did not perform again for almost a week. After this he gave three performances a week, on Monday afternoons and Wednesday and Friday evenings. After two weeks of *Hamlet* he did a week of *King Lear,* then one of *Macbeth,* and eventually added *Romeo and Juliet* to complete his repertoire for this season. As Chatterton had anticipated, the novelty of the unfamiliar foreign star attracted large audiences for at least the early part of the season and, although nothing Rossi offered aroused the enthusiasm which Salvini's *Othello* had stimulated the season before, Rossi continued to attract audiences in reasonable numbers through his two-month engagement. His reception by the London critics was more disappointing, for they were far more severe with him than they had been with Salvini. Even the more favorable reviews, which had some praise for Rossi's technical skill, suggested that in such roles as Hamlet and Lear he was simply inadequate in emotional and intellectual depth. Some, recalling similar complaints about Salvini's Hamlet, suggested that such "northern" characters might be beyond the grasp of Italian actors, whatever their talent. Stung, Rossi wrote a letter to the *Times* following the reviews of his first two offerings insisting that both were based on long and careful reading of the texts and were as legitimate as the traditional English interpretations which his critics were taking as models.[3]

He appears nevertheless to have made some attempt to modify his rather heightened delivery to suit the more conservative English taste, but quite in vain, for subsequent reviews suggested that in so doing he had merely flattened his interpretations and reduced them in interest. Doubtless it was with considerable relief that Rossi closed his season in late June and returned to the more hospitable theatre world of Paris. For his final benefit he offered small samples of two Shakespearian characters he had not played in London—Othello and Shylock. The program was composed of the second acts of *Romeo and Juliet* and *Hamlet*, the third act of *Othello*, and the fourth act of *The Merchant of Venice*.

For the next five years Rossi toured primarily in Europe, gaining particular success in Russia, whither he returned three times. In the meantime, Salvini undertook his first tour to America with a bilingual company, and his success there served, as it had earlier in London, to stimulate a subsequent invitation to Rossi. This time the importance of Salvini's example was even more clear. Rossi was contacted by Charles Chizzola, who had arranged Salvini's first tour to America, and was offered John Stetson's Globe Theatre in Boston as a home theatre there, with essentially the same American company that had just toured with Salvini. Under these arrangements, Rossi arrived in New York in September of 1881, just a few months after Salvini's departure, to spend a short time rehearsing there with his new colleagues before opening in Boston.

External events cast a shadow over this opening. Just as Rossi arrived in New York President Garfield was assassinated, and the unfortunate actor, who had been stranded penniless with his company in Russia the previous year by the assassination of Czar Alexander, had visions of an identical calamity befalling him again. Chizzola, however, was now experienced enough in organizing advance publicity so that interest ran high in the new star despite external events. P. M. Potter in *The Critic* scoffed at these massive publicity campaigns, remarking that Rossi had been "preceded and accompanied by as noisy a crowd of gong-beaters as those who made the name of Sarah Bernhardt odious to quiet theatre-goers."[4] Nevertheless, such campaigns remained effective. New York's black-bordered newspapers gave Rossi excellent coverage, and his opening in Boston was a great success. *Hamlet* and *King Lear,* so indifferently received in London, were here praised to the skies.

Unfortunately this initial enthusiasm did not continue. In New York at the end of October Rossi made the mistake of opening with *Othello,* and the inevitable comparisons with Salvini were never in Rossi's favor. His *Romeo and Juliet* did not fare much better, and not until he finally presented *Hamlet* and *King Lear* did he begin to get stronger reviews. By that time he was drawing very small audiences, perhaps because the public was already sated with bilingual Shakespeare, perhaps because they had decided that the new Italian star was little more than a pale imitation of Salvini. The more favorable reviews he received for *Hamlet* and *King Lear* did not increase his popularity; often an enthusiastic notice would end with a note of regret about the size of his audiences. The *Boston Globe,* which on the whole found Rossi's work superior to Salvini's, found it "difficult to understand" why Rossi could not attract similar houses:

> It is undoubtedly true that the Italian-English style of dramatic representation was very fully exemplified during the Salvini engagements, and probably the public was not altogether disposed to welcome so soon its revival. But it is not creditable to our community, nor does it maintain Boston's reputation as quick to recognize genius, that Rossi should have been so neglected.[5]

Whatever the reason, this pattern of general critical enthusiasm and public indifference continued to plague Rossi in other Eastern cities as he traveled into Canada, through upstate New York, and to Philadelphia.

After Philadelphia, Chizzola booked Rossi into a number of Southern cities—Charleston, Richmond, Savannah, and Atlanta—where neither Ristori nor Salvini had been, perhaps hoping that Rossi would do better with audiences for whom Italian Shakespeare was still a novelty. Matters did not improve; indeed Rossi was forced for the first time to cancel performances because of inadequate sales. In a final attempt to win over the American public, Rossi began to introduce some English into his roles. On 21 December while playing King Lear in Charleston he startled the audience by suddenly crying out in English "Every inch a king" in the fourth act. The audience greeted this innovation with a storm of applause that halted the performance, and Rossi, encouraged, added more lines in English when he appeared in early January in Baltimore and Washington. When he returned to New York in late January, he was able to present the entire final act in English.

In Baltimore, Washington, and New York the addition of English passages, either by their novelty or by their flattery of audience patriotism, succeeded in boosting attendance, but Rossi made slow progress in trying to relearn parts as the tour continued. This is hardly surprising, since his schedule was far more demanding than Salvini's had been. In his 1880–81 tour Salvini regularly performed only on Monday, Wednesday, and Friday evenings with a Saturday matinee, and usually repeated at least one play during the week. Rossi performed daily, and with a larger active repertoire. Typical was his week in Washington, January 9–14: Monday, *Hamlet*; Tuesday and Friday, *Edmund Kean*; Wednesday, *King Lear*; Thursday, *Othello*; Saturday matinee, *Romeo and Juliet*. Sometimes there would be a Saturday evening performance as well. Little wonder that before his departure from New York Rossi commented to a reporter from the *Times* that he considered this tour to have been not only exhausting but actually detrimental to his art.[6]

More discouraging still, when Rossi again went West, to St. Louis, then to Minneapolis and St. Paul, his receipts once again dwindled steadily and alarmingly. He was scheduled to appear in Chicago in mid-February, but by this time the reputation of his tour was such that no theatre manager could be found willing to agree to the conventional arrangement of renting for a certain share of the profits. Finally he appeared at McVicker's, paying a fixed rent of $2,000 a week regardless of income. The end was near. At the beginning of March, in Detroit, Rossi gave up the tour and disbanded the company. Most of them received only enough to pay their fare back to Boston. Rossi himself returned to New York to see what he could arrange through individual bookings. He contracted for a week in Philadelphia later in March, playing *Edmund Kean* for the entire week, with the final scene from *Lear* in English added to two evenings.

In April he was invited to San Francisco by Thomas Maguire, who had sponsored Ristori's San Francisco appearance in 1875. His present theatre, the Baldwin, was on the verge of bankruptcy, and the Rossi booking was Maguire's last desperate attempt to save his venture. He paid the fare of Rossi, two other actors, and a stage manager and supplemented them with the company from the Baldwin. In California Rossi did not have the memory of a previous visit by Salvini to overcome, but this proved no more of an advantage here than it had in the South. He opened with *Othello* and *Hamlet*, which drew average receipts of only about ninety dollars a night. According to the terms of his contract, Rossi kept half of this, leaving little indeed for the rest of the company. Not surprisingly, the rest of the actors and the musicians called a strike, and on 21 April *King Lear* was performed with a total of only four persons in the French and English armies combined.[7] The engagement closed two days later, with *Romeo and Juliet* still in preparation. So ended Rossi's single American tour.

The relative indifference with which he had been greeted was probably initially due in part to the fact that the major cities of the East had already welcomed Ristori and Salvini (the latter the previous season) and were to some extent sated with Italian experimentation and—doubtless equally important—with the now fairly predictable publicity campaigns of the international stars. By the time Rossi reached those cities where his predecessors had not performed he was tired, dispirited, and fighting the word that had already reached these places of his qualified reception in the East. Moreover, he had no single role, like Salvini's Othello or Ristori's Lady Macbeth, upon which he could rely for popular success. In Europe his Hamlet fulfilled this function, but neither English nor American spectators were willing to accept an Italian interpretation of what was

regarded as a quintessentially English or at least Nordic charac-
ter. The conclusion of the review of Rossi's *Hamlet* in the *New
York Tribune* by the highly respected and influential William
Winter clearly demonstrates this conviction:

> These and the other great Shakespearian works exist in their
> integrity nowhere outside of the English language—unless,
> perhaps, in the German. The English ideals of them are the
> right ideals of them, and the English method of acting them
> is the right method. The foreign actors who come here ought
> to deal with what they really understand, and give the great
> works of their own literature, with companies speaking their
> own language.[8]

Such attacks were particularly galling to Rossi because he,
more than either Salvini or Ristori, had based his career on his
interpretations of Shakespeare. The rebuff by English-speaking
audiences hurt him deeply, especially when it was reinforced
by critical comment suggesting that he lacked a real intellectual
grasp of the plays. His extensive Shakespearian commentaries
in *Studii drammatici e Lettere autobiografiche* (Florence, 1885) and
in *Quarant'anni di vita artistica* (Florence, 1887–89) constituted
an impressive refutation of the latter charge, but Rossi never
again submitted his interpretations to the test of presentation
before English-speaking audiences.

Other countries were ready enough, in any case, to welcome
him as one of the great Shakespearian actors of the period. He
even played bilingual Shakespeare, with great success, in Swe-
den and in Germany. He was invited to participate in a Goethe
festival at Weimar and to play Othello, Lear, and Hamlet with
the famous company of the Duke of Saxe-Meiningen. In 1886
he toured Italy with his own translation of *Julius Caesar*. His
final tours were to Turkey, Greece, and to Russia, where in 1896
as he was performing *King Lear* he was stricken with the illness
which led to his death in Italy soon after.

11
Rossi's *Hamlet*

Critical reaction to Rossi's *Hamlet* varied more widely than the reaction to any role in Salvini's repertoire. This may be partly explained by the fact that Rossi was much more willing than Salvini to experiment with his roles, retaining the most striking effects and the overall contours of a production, but otherwise frequently altering rhythms, moods, and the emphases of various scenes. Moreover *Hamlet*, which he considered and most critics acknowledged to be the keystone of his repertoire, corresponding to Salvini's *Othello*, suffered as *Othello* did not from the inevitable comparisons with an already firmly established image of the role. This was particularly the case in London and was remarked upon by several journals. The *Pall Mall Budget*, for example, suggested that Rossi was "not well advised" to appear first as Hamlet:

> Our idea of the Prince of Denmark is such that, unless we are previously familiar with the person of the actor, and have therefore prepared our minds for a slight shock, the presence of a new comer on the stage in the well-known sable suit too often gives rise to disappointment. . . . Thus from the time when Signor Rossi first comes forward there is a prejudice to overcome which would scarcely have been equally felt in any other character.[1]

The *Athenæum* admitted that the view of Hamlet which had been established by generations of English actors might in fact not be correct, but that it was nevertheless the view which the English playgoer assumed as given when he went to the theatre. Rossi, though "a trained and accomplished actor, with a wide range of powers," unfortunately had developed "a theory of Hamlet which to Englishmen is wholly unintelligible."[2]

In America Rossi fared much better at the hands of the critics, especially early in his tour. The reviewer from the *Boston Globe* on 7 October 1881 went so far in his enthusiasm as to call Rossi's Hamlet "one of the finest that this country has ever seen." He flatly denied the suggestion repeatedly aired in London that Italian actors were perhaps incapable of portraying this role and argued, on the contrary, that "the superior mobility of countenance and flexibility of person characteristic of the Latin race" gave them a decided advantage. "Every emotion and impulse of their tempestuous temperaments naturally betrays itself through limb and features. Pre-eminently is this the case with Signor Rossi, and the fitful moods of Hamlet enable him to make the most of his remarkable power." Rossi had a further edge over his countryman Salvini, since the latter had gained much of his effect through sheer massiveness and physical power, while Rossi's talent was more subtle. Clearly he possessed "in a very high degree that refinement of intellect which alone can master complex creations like Hamlet."

Other American critics tended to take positions of less unqualified enthusiasm, but most considered Rossi's Hamlet his best role and this production one of major importance. It was Rossi's misfortune that this reaction had little effect on the general public; often a review full of warm praise closed on a note of regret that the audience had been so sparse. The praise too became somewhat more guarded as the tour began to founder, until Rossi's last American reviews were almost as discouraging as any he had received in London. William Winter, summing up his interpretation, said flatly that he "did not and could not look like Hamlet, and considered according to the English-speaking or -reading standard relative to Shakespeare's tragedy, he did not and could not act Hamlet."[3]

The version of the play which Rossi presented was much closer to the original than Salvini's. It was based on the prose translation of Rusconi, but corrected by Rossi's own study of the play and by comparison with the Kean promptbook. This gave a better approximation of the play (at least in overall structure) than the Salvini version, though there was not much improvement line by line for those who understood Italian. The Italian-English libretti sold at the theatres only emphasized the problem, since the anonymous English translator seemingly could not decide whether to follow literally the rather flat Italian or to slip into the familiar Shakespearian lines. Thus "Io, si, e con me Marcello" was rendered into the peculiar but vaguely Shakespearian "A piece of him, and Marcellus also," while Shakespeare's line "Shall I strike at it with my partisan?" which in the Italian version became "Debbo dargli sulla testa?" came back into English as the unadorned "Shall I knock him on the head?"

The examples are both, of course, from Shakespeare's opening scene, which Salvini had cut but which Rossi included. Rossi's first appearance, in the court scene which followed, was something of a shock, particularly in England. He was a short, burly man, and his dress and bearing, far from deemphasizing his stocky frame, clearly were meant to suggest the "adipose" Hamlet mentioned by Salvini. The critics who had been disturbed by Salvini's large, physically powerful Hamlet were outraged by this much less impressive departure from the thin and delicate prince of tradition. "The condition of fatness is at variance with all the characteristics of Hamlet, physical and mental," huffed William Winter. "No reasonable person wants blubber with the melancholy Dane."[4]

Still, Rossi was normally anything but lymphatic. He shared with Salvini a flair for the physical, and his most effective scenes were those in which he gave full rein to his mobile features and expressive gestures. Unfortunately, very little of this appeared in his first scene in *Hamlet,* which he played in a key of unrelieved and quiet gloom, giving a rather unimpressive beginning to his interpretation. Nothing lightened or varied the scene even for a moment, complained the *Saturday Review.* "His reception of Horatio, 'I know you are no truant,' is so profoundly melancholy that he seems to be in mourning for his friend's industrious disposition, and even the excitement of hearing that his father's ghost has appeared hardly makes a break in the monotony of his despair."[5] Rossi apparently took this criticism to heart, for on his American tour he reacted to the news of the ghost violently, with a start almost as violent as Salvini's backward leap and no less strong than his later reaction upon encountering the ghost itself. This sacrificed any subtlety on the "Saw? Who?" but did provide a strong theatrical effect in the otherwise subdued scene.

The scene on the ramparts allowed Rossi much more variety and action and as a result was distinctly more successful. Rossi, like Salvini, had an impressive vocal range, which he emphasized by abrupt shifts in volume and tone. Thus after the thrilling cry "Angels and ministers of grace defend us!" he dropped at once to an awed and reverent half-whisper for "Be thou a spirit of health or goblin damned." Particular lines, such as "O my prophetic soul! My uncle!" were given with chilling intensity; indeed, Rossi seems to have relied heavily upon the device of giving selected lines with particular force rather than gradually building up an effect. On seeing the ghost he fell backward with a wild cry, and his portrayal of fearful reverence as the spirit addressed him was considered highly effective. When the ghost disappeared, he fell flat to the ground and delivered part of the following speech in that position. When he arose, the madness had come to the fore, so that even the speech "O all ye host of heaven," before the return of Hamlet's friends, seemed composed of "wild and whirling words." The interchange with Horatio and the others was much reduced, though Rossi still retained much more of it than Salvini had. "You'll reveal it" became a simple "Non posso" (I cannot) and the "There's ne'er a villain" speech and response were gone. Part of the swearing scene was removed also, but Rossi, unlike Salvini and indeed unlike most of the English actors of the period, kept enough of the "fellow in the cellerage" to give an idea of the whole and to create a striking impression of a wild nervous excitement in Hamlet. The act ended with the tableau of the swearing, requiring the cutting of Hamlet's final speech.

During the second act Rossi's interpretation diverged much more sharply from Salvini's. The ironical, even savage humor of Hamlet which Salvini chose to suppress Rossi emphasized, reinforcing it with such violence of gesture and expression that many critics felt he was more thoroughly the madman than any other Hamlet of recent memory. Some, such as the *Pall Mall Budget*, felt that this destroyed the dignity of the character: "his dress neglected, his speech rough, and his whole manner boorish."[6] Others, like the *New York Tribune*, found this approach impressive and even moving:

> In act second it was quite impossible to tell whether the actor's intention was to depict the madness as real or assumed; but, either way, it was depicted with fidelity to truth, and with much beauty of detail, throughout the colloquies with the two courtiers and Polonius. Signor Rossi's management of his eyes is here notably fine, and the misery underlying an air of grotesque mystery and sardonic humor had an effect of rare pathos.[7]

The scene of Hamlet's banter with Polonius was generally admired in Rossi's production. There was a delicate mixture of weariness and whimsy, half real and half assumed, given with much truth to nature. Particularly striking was Rossi's reading of "Words, words, words," in which, said the *Academy*, "the first utterance conveys irritation, and the second regret, and the third (said in a calmed undertone) the necessary resignation that such emptiness must be."[8] Perhaps the most unusual feature of this scene was that Rossi had Rosencrantz and Guildenstern on stage during the entire Hamlet-Polonius interchange, and Polonius delivered to them such traditional asides as "Still harping on my daughter" and "Though this be madness, yet there is method in't." In the following scene with these two courtiers Rossi received some complaint for too much sameness in his playing. Not only did he clearly mistrust these friends, but he showed them unmistakably from the beginning that he did so. He knitted his brows, glared at them suspiciously, addressed them in tones of sarcastic reproach. There was no room for the heartfelt appeal to a former comradeship which most Hamlets have used in the attempt to determine their present loyalty.

In the first scene with the players, Rossi used the same odd and quite unjustified interpretation Salvini had used for

Polonius's "Look, whether he has not turned his color," making it refer to Hamlet rather than to the player. In Rossi's case, clearly this was to provide himself with an opportunity to make one of the sudden emotional transitions which were one of his most effective theatrical devices. Another such abrupt change, and a much more legitimate one, came in the following soliloquy, which is clearly written for an abrupt transition after "O vengeance!" Rossi built up to this emotional peak with much beating of the head and tearing of the hair, then cried out "O—O—Vendetta!" at the footlights, full front, with arms spread wide (a favorite gesture of his), before dropping back to introspective realism. The shift was praised even by those generally critical of his performance, and the quiet but emotional delivery he gave to the remaining lines of the soliloquy gave them a poetic resonance which some considered equal to the original. This act invariably concluded with tumultuous applause.

The "To be or not to be" speech was perhaps Rossi's closest moment to the Hamlet of tradition, but it was for that reason less distinctly his own and not generally considered especially striking or memorable. Its perfect elocution and melodious beauty were often praised, though some critics suggested that Rossi's Hamlet did not seem enough of a thinker to frame such a soliloquy. The confrontation with Ophelia drew strikingly mixed reactions. Rossi, even more than Salvini, departed completely from the tradition which gave a coarse, even brutal edge to this scene. His words were cruel, but delivered with a despairing tenderness that revealed his own agony. The *Charleston News and Courier* of 21 December 1881 considered Rossi warmer, more genuine, and softer than any other major actor of Hamlet and felt this scene the key one in creating that effect. On the other hand, Rossi was given to introducing odd bits of business into this scene, which caused some puzzlement and complaint. Hamilton Aïdé in the *Academy* remarked that on Ophelia's entry Rossi went up to her and at once laid his hand on the casket she was carrying. "His motive for this action I cannot conceive, as it weakens all that follows."[9] On the line "Where's your father?" Rossi, with no warning, leaped to an upstage center door and flung it open, crying, presumably after Polonius's retreating figure, "Let the doors be shut upon him."

He then slammed the door and returned to Ophelia, abruptly resuming his tone of suffering sadness as if nothing had happened. Nor did Ophelia herself give any reaction to this jolting interruption.

Rossi, unlike Salvini, performed the advice to the players scene, giving it a quiet, relaxed tone which aroused little enthusiasm in the reviewers but which, like his other quiet scenes, prepared by contrast for a coming sequence of high emotionality. This was the play within the play scene, which Rossi performed in a highly agitated manner. "Here is a man in such a violent stage of lunacy that nothing short of a strait-waistcoat or a padded room is appropriate to his condition," said the *Pall Mall Budget*. "He lies down at Ophelia's feet and rolls and kicks about in a manner so grotesque that the King would have wanted no better excuse than this conduct to get rid of him at once."[10] As the King rose and fled, Rossi blocked his exit, fiercely scanning his face as Claudius cried out for light. Hamlet's wild reaction after the court has left, omitted by Salvini, was emphasized by Rossi, who leaped onto the throne, kicking both legs up into the air, clapping his hands in delight and shouting "è vero—è vero!" After his London opening, when the exuberance of this particular moment aroused general protest, Rossi assumed the throne with more dignity, but toned down little else in the sequence. Nor did he adjust what the *Saturday Review* characterized as his "excessively tiresome habit of beginning and interrupting every one of his speeches with variously intoned exclamations of ah! and eh!"[11]

After the violent reading of this scene, Rossi again clearly sought an effect of sharp contrast by shifting to his quiet, intense delivery for the recorder scene, which he retained, and the scene in the King's closet. English Hamlets usually carried on Hamlet's state of high excitement after the play into the recorder scene, so Rossi's calm delivery, marked only by a subdued laugh at the end as he returned the instrument to Rosencrantz, was something of a surprise to his audiences. One curious reading was the line "There is much music, excellent voice, in this little organ; yet cannot you make it speak," during which Rossi slapped his chest as though it were his own voice and not the recorder being spoken of.

In his comments on the play Rossi mentions the opening scene on the ramparts and the King's prayer scene as sequences so critical to the play that only a "vandal" would consider omitting them.[12] In fact both were frequently heavily cut if not removed entirely, and Rossi deserves credit for realizing their importance. Aïdé felt that Rossi's performance of the scene in the King's closet was the peak of his interpretation:

> The expression of Rossi's face, the arrested movement on the words "Rientra nel fodero O mia spada" [Back into your scabbard, my sword] were poetical in the highest degree. The great dramatist's outline was nobly filled up; the irresolution, the sorrowful self-contempt, the dread of committing murder at such a moment were finely indicated; the picture of his figure as he lingered at the door is not easily to be forgotten.[13]

In the scene with Gertrude, Rossi returned to a more violent and erratic reading. His killing of Polonius was condemned by many reviewers as crude and melodramatic, and his treatment of Gertrude was little better received. The *Saturday Review* remarked that his entreaty to her to repent was given with true feeling but that it was "difficult to admire the brutality with which he drags her about the stage."[14] When the ghost appeared, Rossi ducked behind a chair and continued to dodge away from the phantom, even creeping around to hide behind the Queen. "Nothing more ignoble can be conceived," was the judgement of Aïdé.[15] More likely Rossi simply saw the scene as presenting an opportunity to display the rapid changes of mood at which he excelled, an excellent showcase for his Hamlet's whimsical instability, if not outright madness. He restored the almost universally cut lines about the birds flying and the "famous ape"—presumably so that he could pantomime the actions of this metaphorical menagerie. The *New York Herald* remarked on his proclivity for gestural language:

> So much time did Rossi consume in pantomime between lines, and even words, that in spite of his rapid reading and the fact that the performance began promptly on time and

the "waits" were not longer than usual, the curtain did not fall until a few minutes before midnight.[16]

Rossi felt that the sequence with the portraits was the high point of this scene and accordingly moved it to the scene's conclusion. He managed the portraits in a more conventional way than Salvini, by means of lockets hung about his own neck and Gertrude's, but added his own distinctive touch to this business by tearing the Queen's locket from her neck, dashing it to the floor, and dancing upon it in maniacal triumph—a piece of business warmly applauded by the public and almost universally condemned by the reviewers. Immediately after, he showed Hamlet struck by a sort of childish repentance and falling weeping at his mother's knee, upon which emotional tableau the act ended.

Like Salvini, Rossi moved rapidly, with much cutting, through the final two acts. Neither Signora Cattaneo in London or Louise Muldener in America was particularly strong as Ophelia, and the mad scene, much cut and with all singing omitted, made little impression. In his own commentaries on the play Rossi observed that the churchyard scene caused him the most difficulties in interpretation, and that indeed he did not first understand it until he was standing in the wings in Milan, ready to perform it for the first time. Then it suddenly occurred to him that in this scene Hamlet comes to the realization that his true home is the grave. A shudder ran through him, and the playing of the scene became natural and easy.[17] Unfortunately, the revelation Rossi felt seems not to have had much effect on English audiences, perhaps because of the difficulty of conveying anything of the verbal sparring with the gravedigger through another language. For most observers, Rossi seemed merely to be shifting back to an air of solemnity and restraint after the passion in which he had last been observed, and some even felt the colloquy with the gravedigger had rather an air of dullness and preaching about it. The tension began to mount again with Ophelia's burial, which was much cut and rapidly rushed through. In England Rossi's subdued delivery appears to have affected even the grappling with Laertes, in which he was accused of a want of passion, but

American reviewers generally characterized his performance in this sequence as "powerful" and "manly."

The hint of approaching catastrophe which Shakespeare expressed in the short scene between Horatio and Hamlet containing the "readiness is all" speech Rossi converted into a virtual certainty by the following interchange, inserted immediately before the duel:

Horatio: My Lord, please do not.
Hamlet: My friend, honor compels me, but if I am betrayed, none will enjoy my death.

This interpolation was particularly odd since Rossi, perhaps in reaction to the charge of Italianate plotting brought against Salvini's Hamlet, insisted that even when Hamlet exchanges foils with Laertes he is still unaware of the treachery about him—a degree of naiveté most unusual in Hamlet interpretation:

Hamlet does not wound Laertes on purpose. He does not know the blades have been tampered with. He does not even realize, in the heat of the fighting, that he himself has been wounded. He knows nothing of all this until Laertes tells him.[18]

On the other hand, Laertes's awareness was made much more obvious than usual by the following interpolated exchange after the change of weapons:

Laertes: Why, you give me your foil.
Hamlet: Yes.
Laertes: I am lost.

As soon as Laertes revealed the treachery to him, Rossi rushed upon the King, tossing his foil up into the air, catching it by the middle, and then using it as a dagger to plunge into Claudius's body. He then forced the King to drink from the poisoned goblet, an action both surprising and shocking for English and American audiences, who had never seen this gesture, nor heard the line "Drink off this potion" presented on the English-speaking stage. No critic praised the restoration (indeed none seems to have recognized it as a restoration) and most considered it grotesque or unfortunately comic. One said it suggested the dosing of a refractory child.

Rossi then, for the second time in the play, staggered to the throne, where he delivered his final speech. In his commentary on *Hamlet* he expressed his opinion that Hamlet would have been a poor king, indecisive and weak. Thus Shakespeare introduced Fortinbras to assure his monarchic audiences that the throne would survive. Fortinbras did not appear in Rossi's version, but the prince's final speech provided for him to assume the throne, and his impending arrival was suggested by the sound of martial music from offstage. With the line "The rest is silence" the play ended.

12
Rossi's *King Lear*

The critical reaction to Rossi's *King Lear*, taken as a whole, suggests that it was distinctly better received than his *Hamlet*, though there was a similar difference between English and American reviewers. The unqualified enthusiasm which the *Boston Globe* expressed for *Hamlet* was not widely echoed in the American press, but similar accolades for *King Lear* were fairly common. The rapture of the *New York Times* was not at all atypical:

> It was the most perfect and comprehensive Shakespearian performance that we have ever seen or expect to see. It had the power of vast passion subjected to a lofty and elastic art; it had the beauty of a rounded and harmonious finish, combined with the most intensive feeling and the most heartbreaking pathos; it lacked nothing that belongs to either life or art, and as a work shaped out of the very flesh and spirit of man it was simply pre-eminent.[1]

Nothing of this sort appeared in the London reviews, but there too Rossi's Lear was distinctly preferred to his Hamlet. The general opinion seems to have been that in terms of acting technique the Italian actor's achievement was outstanding, but that he neither touched the soul of the character nor attempted to express the subtleties revealed by generations of English actors and scholars. The complaint was raised that Rossi never got beyond the limits of "mere acting." The *Athenæum* reported that "though the powers of the actor are remarkable, and are such as especially commend themselves to the more highly trained portion of his audience, the result to the student, at least, is blank disappointment."[2]

Rossi's first appearance as Lear was one of his most impressive. He seemed a powerful and picturesque, semi-barbaric figure, with a massive gray beard and shock of gray hair, his dress rich and striking. Still, he did not move with the power and authority which many actors of Lear, including Salvini, felt was essential to the opening scene. Rossi played no slightly enfeebled titan, but an old man, clearly in his dotage, whose movements were lacking not in grace but certainly in authority. Vocally too he avoided the powerful effects of which he was capable, modulating his speech to suggest the tones of a man of great years tossed on a sea of contending and confusing emotion. Even his bursts of rage at Cordelia and Kent seemed merely senile outbursts, brief and rather pathetic. The London *Times* of 5 May 1876 called him "too querulous, too evidently in his dotage" and suggested that thereby Rossi had lost all impression of Lear's kingly dignity. The actor responded, in some pique, that the opening scene, with the division of the kingdom, the foolish test upon which it is based, and Lear's extreme reaction to Cordelia's refusal to participate—all were compatible with his view of Lear as a man whose wits were already failing at the beginning of the play.[3] One effect of this interpretation was to give a certain sameness to each of Lear's outbursts, so that the rage at Cordelia and Kent was very similar to that displayed subsequently toward the uncivil Oswald and again in the climactic confrontation with Goneril.

The curse speech, to which Salvini had given such titanic force, was delivered by Rossi in a far more subtle and subdued manner. During the interview with his daughter leading up to it, he suggested the slipping away of his reason by a powerful display of erratic conflicting emotions, by turns sarcastic, appealing, angry, and tearful. The *Academy* particularly admired a touch just before the curse:

This was a restless unconscious survey of Goneril, with rapid glances at her feet, thence carried upward slowly to the head, as if his daughter, thus transformed in his eyes, must necessarily reveal some outward characteristic of the inward change; or as if there were still some half-formed hope of discovering proof that the whole scene was unreal.[4]

Rossi launched into "Detested kite! Thou liest" with a passion that suggested he would follow the general custom of delivering this entire speech with furious intensity. But concentration of this sort was quite beyond the Lear he was creating, and the reference to Cordelia, only a few lines later, was delivered in a totally contrasting tone, with a profoundly affecting break in his voice. When he rushed from the stage in anguish, there was little doubt that his curse had been an admission of powerlessness and of defeat.

The rest of the act was omitted, though Rossi retained the two lines following Lear's exit so that the act in fact ended with Goneril's advice to Albany: "But let his disposition have that scope that dotage gives it." Clearly Rossi retained these lines to reinforce the idea of Lear's senility, or even of his madness, at this early point in the play, since in the Italian all references to dotage were translated as "pazzia" or "follia." The other major cuts in the first act were Edmund's "This is the excellent foppery of the world" speech, most of the jests of the fool, the opening dialogue between Kent and Gloucester, and the entire sequence between the entrance of France and Burgundy and France's acceptance of Cordelia.

During the second act, the progress of Lear's degeneration became more marked by physical symptoms. In the first act Rossi's hands had trembled and his head twitched and wagged. To these were now added a half-opened mouth, a vacant stare, and a hesitating voice. Occasionally these symptoms would briefly disappear as Lear would make an abortive attempt to recover from the stupor he felt creeping upon him, but a relapse would always quickly follow. There was much more of confusion and offended dignity than of anger in his confrontation with Regan, and he begged her almost childishly for kinder treatment than he had received from her sister. At the appearance of Goneril his quick anger flared up, but as always dissolved almost at once into pathetic mumblings. Some of Rossi's most effective moments in this act came when the lines reinforced this sort of rapid shift from angry resolution to confused hesitation. His sudden check as he was about to send a violent message to the Duke was one example. Another, deeply pathetic, was his change of mood on "I will do such things,—what they are, yet I know not. . . ." A small but significant adjustment was made in Regan's line "I pray you father, being weak, seem so" by the insertion of "di mente" (of mind) after weak, changing Shakespeare's clear emphasis on Lear's loss of authority to a comment on his failing mental powers. The end of this act (which Rossi, like Salvini, concluded with the "O, reason not the need" speech) was, like the end of the first act, played for its quiet emotion rather than for its passion. The *Boston Globe* called the delivery of these lines a model of "the height of power in pathos:"

> The actor seemed lost in the part, and we saw only the wretched Lear as full of grief as age. Attitude, voice, mien, all added to the effect of the moving portrayal, and the artist was recalled, amid the heartiest applause of the evening.[5]

The heath scenes, a disappointment in Salvini's *King Lear*, were considered among Rossi's best. The technical effects of the storm were generally judged impressive and suitable, as Salvini's were not, but much more important, of course, was Rossi's own approach to these critical scenes. In his view it was not until this point in the play, when the loss of his royal power is fully realized even amid the overthrow of his reason, that Lear's true kingly dignity appears. Thus, without losing the pathos of earlier scenes nor the carefully studied symptoms of madness, Rossi now began to give to his Lear a stature which he had previously lacked. The London *Times*, which complained of precisely this "want of dignity" in the opening scenes, grudgingly admitted that Rossi became "more kingly in his insanity" and that in the heath scenes

Signor Rossi was perhaps at his best, partly because the extravagance in which he is so prone to indulge was here more in harmony with the spirit of the scene, and partly too, because he, much to our astonishment, held that extravagance well in check.[6]

Rossi's madness was already too well established before the entrance of Edgar as "poor Tom" to suggest that the pretended madman led his wits any further astray, but the hallucinatory quality of the Tom scene was nevertheless given particular power in Rossi's interpretation. The *St. Louis Globe-Democrat* called the meeting of the madmen in the midst of the storm

> a weird and wonderful piece of work, novel and surprising in its effect and stripped of the traditions to which English-speaking tragedians still cling. The very movements of the actor, the strange swayings of his body as he went through the scene following the phantoms conjured up for him by Tom, were revelations concerning the part that few in the audience were prepared for.[7]

In the mock trial, Rossi again avoided the rage which normally accompanied the cursing of the unnatural daughters, drawing instead upon an intensity of feeling more original, more suited to the scene he had created, and surely more effective in this interpretation. He continued to break sequences of high intensity, even more sharply than in earlier acts. Moy Thomas, writing in the *Academy*, observed:

> Signor Rossi seems to have made of the characteristics of madness a special study; he has a remarkable faculty for indicating by his features the rapid changes of mood and the points at which the mind becomes suddenly occupied by new ideas; and at no time does he win more pity for the poor, forlorn, ill-used, despised old king than when, from a fit of high philosophizing or indignant complaint, he lapses into the happy vacant smiles of a mind too much shaken for continuous effort.[8]

By the end of this act Rossi's Lear seemed almost totally exhausted, and in a moment of great tenderness the fool, humoring his notion that he is going to bed, encouraged the old king to sink down into his arms and into tranquil sleep. The fool's final line, "And I'll go to bed at noon," cut by Salvini, was retained by Rossi to finish this tableau and the act.

With a few minor exceptions, Rossi's cuts in the first three acts followed those of Salvini, but their versions of the final acts were more distinct. Salvini began his fourth act with the traditional act 4, scene 2, while Rossi began with the opening lines of act 3, scene 8, in which Oswald reveals to Cornwall and the sisters that Lear has departed for Dover. The actual blinding of Gloucester which follows was omitted by Rossi as it had been by Salvini, though when Gloucester appeared in the next scene his makeup suggested with grim realism eyesockets from which the eyes had been torn. This scene was much reduced, all of the lines between Gloucester's meeting with his son and "Dost thou know Dover?" being omitted. Scenes 2, 3, 4, and 5 were cut, along with the beginning of scene 6, containing the false suicide on Dover Cliff. Thus the first Edgar-Gloucester scene led directly into the encounter with the mad king decked with flowers. During the first part of his American tour, Rossi had nothing in this scene to compare with the effect of Salvini's famous seizing of a branch as scepter, but, when he began to convert parts of the play into English, he began with the single line "Every inch a king" and thus created a considerable sensation. Gradually he added subsequent speeches and at length offered the entire last act in English. The *New York Herald* of 18 January 1882 reported that the actor's shift into English late in the play met with "hearty and admiring response" from an audience "who were fairly electrified by a patriotic or egotistical enthusiasm."

Rossi, like Salvini, cut the beginning and end of act 4, scene 7, so that the scene began with Cordelia's "How does the King?" and ended with "Pray you now, forget and forgive; I am old and foolish." The recognition of Cordelia in this scene was one of Rossi's finest and most moving moments, and critics often remarked that in power and pathos Rossi surpassed even

Salvini's much-praised rendering of this moment. The recognition came upon Rossi's Lear gradually. He first rose from his couch to greet this unknown lady, then regarded her in confusion, finally, as she knelt before him, recognized her. He then gently raised her to her feet, clasped her beloved head in his hands, then sank himself to his knees, lifting his trembling hands for forgiveness, a tableau called indescribably tender and touching. Said William Winter:

> The forlorn behavior, the enfeebled body, the wistful countenance, the imploring gaze, the quavering voice, the trembling hands, the manner of mingled mental wandering and hesitant intelligence,—these were affecting constituents of a piteous image of human misery.[9]

In the final act Rossi played the first two scenes, shifted about and reduced by Salvini, in their original form. In the scene with Lear and Cordelia as captives and the death scene Rossi was considered less successful than in the universally praised recognition scene. In the captive scene the actor lost some of the pathos and calm resignation offered by the situation by reverting to an echo of his old imperious manner of anger and senile defiance on such lines as "He that parts us shall bring a brand from heaven, / And fire us hence like foxes."

No such truculent or violent note touched the final scene though Thomas called it "too painful to contemplate for harmonious effect." In any case, when Rossi began to perform these closing scenes in English, this proved such a distraction that few observers seem to have paid much attention to anything else he was doing. Most critics agreed that Rossi's English was accurate and distinct, if somewhat labored. Not all applauded the change; some remarked on a certain loss of expressiveness and emotional focus when Rossi shifted to English, and others a loss of beauty. The *New York Herald* of 18 January 1882 complained that when Rossi "abandoned his mother tongue for the harsher language of his audience there was a discordance in it that made it indeed like the sound of 'sweet bells jangled out of tune.' " All critics agreed, however, that, whatever its difficulties, this innovation was enthusiastically received by the general public. The play ended with Lear's final speech, "Look there, look there!"

13
Rossi's *Othello*

S ince Rossi performed only the third act of *Othello* in London, during his final benefit, we must rely entirely upon reports from American observers as to his interpretation and its effect upon English-speaking audiences. Inevitably, of course, Rossi was compared with Salvini in this role, not only in general interpretation, but in scene-by-scene detail. Considering Salvini's enormous success as Othello, it is hardly surprising that Rossi normally suffered in these comparisons, but his interpretation still received much praise, and in certain scenes he was in fact widely conceded to be superior to his countryman.

The two Othellos were generally judged to be products of the same school, a school which made the character more passionate, more vigorous, more realistic in detail, more given to expressive facial and physical gesture than English or American Othellos. The major difference between the two Italians seemed to be in the lightness or polish of the character. Rossi gave little of the effect of the untamed savage or ferocious animal so often suggested by Salvini. He was more the courtly soldier, with greater decorum and sensitivity to the social situation and the feelings of others. The *Toronto Globe* of 12 November 1881 said "Rossi has the advantage in grace and vivacity, Salvini excelled in simplicity and force."

Rossi played the first act almost uncut, restoring the opening scene which Salvini always omitted. He made himself much

155

more a blackamoor than Salvini, but except for coloring his skin, he used little makeup. His face was open and pleasant, though there was a hint of the barbaric in his colorful costume and his expansive gestures. He played in a lower key generally than Salvini, not without energy but with a sort of buoyant, good-natured, happy-go-lucky spirit which gave a much lighter (and some felt more trivial) tone to the encounter with Brabantio and to the scene in the Senate. Rossi did not bring to this latter scene the variety of gesture and expression Salvini had, and in comparison with his countryman was often judged rather uninteresting, especially in the sequence before his defense. The *New York World* remarked that while Brabantio was pouring out his abuse, Rossi's face expressed "nothing more than good-humoured dullness."

Othello's defense Rossi delivered, oddly enough, directly toward the audience, with his back to the Doge and Senators. His gestures were considered restless and flippant, but his voice was commended as his most effective weapon. It had a natural, loverlike earnestness and a soft musicality which made the wooing perfectly believable, even if it did not seem entirely appropriate to the recounting of "hair-breadth scapes i' the imminent deadly breach." The parting speech of Brabantio, "Look to her, Moor," which Salvini received as a thunderbolt, indeed the first goad to his jealousy, Rossi received calm and smiling, apparently secure in the loyalty and faithfulness of his new wife.

Most reviewers of Rossi's *Othello* reported that through the second act he maintained his graceful and courtly air, suggesting little of the ferocity of Salvini either in love, when he welcomed Desdemona to Cyprus, or in anger, when he upbraided Cassio about the brawl in the streets. The major exception to this opinion was the *New York Herald*, which reported that

> the greeting to Desdemona, at Cyprus, was accompanied with a gloating animalism that is utterly out of place, whether in the character or in the scene. Old Volpone himself could not be more lewd that this Othello was, with his rolling eyes and uxorious exultation. The rebuke of Cassio had rage enough, but no nobleness and no sorrow.[1]

One might be tempted to assume from this that Rossi, who was much more likely than Salvini to experiment with his roles, was on this occasion playing more broadly than was his wont, but the *New York World*, reviewing the same performance, said that Rossi maintained a "quiet demeanor" throughout the second act, "expressing occasional gleams of intelligence and dignity." Perhaps the *Herald* reviewer found the facial and gestural expression to which Rossi was inclined more suggestive than these were intended to be or, more likely, he was simply overreacting to realistic touches in an interpretation which he characterized in general as "unpoetic, un-Shakespearian, and unpleasant." Rossi's major cuts in this act were the badinage between Iago and Desdemona in the first scene and the opening of the third scene, up to the entrance of Cassio. The act ended with Iago's soliloquy "And what's he then that says I play the villain?" reduced to about half its original length.

Rossi followed the usual practice of omitting the two brief opening scenes of the third act and beginning with Cassio's conversation with Desdemona. Iago's first hints to Othello came next and, despite the open and relaxed manner of Rossi's Othello up to this point, he responded to these hints with a rapidity even greater than Salvini's. As early as "Thou dost mean something" there was an insinuation which almost gave the impression that Othello already suspected the subject of Iago's hinting and was eager to draw him out. This impression was emphasized by the fact that Rossi used no business like Salvini's paperwork to provide a distraction for himself. He gave Iago his undivided attention from the outset and thus seemed, as the *San Francisco Chronicle* of 16 April 1882 observed, "to be on stage for the purpose of being made jealous." When Desdemona returned, Rossi was already so convinced of her infidelity that he reacted to her with much greater brutality than Salvini had. As she moved to embrace him and bind his forehead, he recoiled violently from her with a sudden, inexpressible horror, a piece of business much admired.

Like Salvini, Rossi built himself into a ferocity of hate and vengeance as Iago continued to work upon him, until this burst forth in a violent attack on his tormentor. He seized Iago by the throat and bore him to the ground, shaking him savagely, his own head keeping time with this movement. Then, dragging him again to his feet, he cast him away furiously, much as Salvini did. This sort of attack, considered so effective in Salvini's interpretation, was notably less successful in the context of a generally less passionate and savage Othello, however, and Rossi was often criticized for being too violent and sensational at this point. "The great point," said Henry James,

> was his seizing Iago's head and whacking it half-a-dozen times on the floor, and then flinging him twenty years away. It was wonderfully done, but in the doing of it and in the evident relish for it in the house there was I scarce know what force of easy and thereby rather cheap expression.[2]

Just before Rossi's arrival in San Francisco, the *Chronicle* printed a report on the rehearsal of this scene at the Baldwin Theatre. Despite the exaggeration for comic effect, it does indicate both Rossi's approach to the scene and an American response. The reporter arrives on stage to find Joseph Grismer, the leading man of the Baldwin, being shaken and choked by the Italian stage manager, representing Rossi:

> "Yes, yes," ejaculated Grismer, between his chokes, "but where's the cue?"
> "Yar waita," said the Italian gentleman. . . "Yar waita till I knocka yar head on the stage, then tat is the cuea."
> Grismer shook himself together. "Is Signor Rossi much more muscular than you?" asks Joseph.
> "He is moocha more stronga."
> "Then there won't be any need for a cue. They'll want another Iago for the last act," exclaimed the disgruntled Grismer.
> The rehearsal proceeded. The representative of Signor Rossi spoke in Italian and the other actors in English, the dialogue running something as follows:
> Othello's proxy (laying his hand on the curve of his vest)—Addio—el tranquilo mondo addio contento, addio da capo troopa, anda da granda fighta o—o—oo . . . Othello est veto—oo—o—o!
> Grismer (furtively measuring the distance between the stage

manager and the prompter's table)—I am sorry to hear
this, my lord.

Othello's proxy—Villeano—o, vi—lean—o? (Makes a dash at
Grismer and catches the agile Iago before he can dodge
around the prompter's table, grasps him by the throat and
shakes him till his teeth rattle).

Grismer (in gasps)—Y-e-s, my lud—You're eaten up with
passion.[3]

Rossi, like Salvini, ended the third act with the vows of
Othello and Iago, and began his fourth act with the traditional
act 4, scene 4. The *Toronto Globe* of 17 November 1881 reported
that Rossi cut this scene, in which Othello demands the handkerchief from Desdemona, but if so it was a temporary and
rather peculiar experiment which he seemingly did not repeat
elsewhere. Normally he played the scene with essentially the
same cuts as Salvini, ending it at the entrance of Cassio and
Iago. Again like Salvini, Rossi omitted the epileptic seizure, but
the following sequence, in which Othello listens to the conversation between Cassio and Iago, never given by Salvini, was
restored by Rossi and well received. This choice was probably
made in keeping with Rossi's interest in making the sources of
Othello's jealousy as palpable and certain as possible.

In the sequence with Lodovico, the sorrow and shame which
Salvini emphasized became for Rossi contempt and loathing for
the woman whose corruption had just been revealed to him.
His outstanding moment in this scene was when at Lodovico's
request he called Desdemona back. Thinking he was about to
give her a kind word, she rushed toward him, only to have him
shrink back in repulsion and gesture for her to join Lodovico.
The second half of act 4, scene 2 (in which Iago, Desdemona,
and Emilia discuss the change which has come over Othello),
which Salvini played next, Rossi omitted entirely so that there
remained in the fourth act only the furious scene between
Othello and Desdemona which ends with Othello's exit "I pray
you, turn the key, and keep our counsel." Here Rossi ended
this act.

Both Rossi and Salvini began their final act with the traditional act 4, scene 3 though Rossi omitted more of the scene, including Emilia's last long speech. Indeed, Emilia's role was much reduced throughout the final act. The attack on Cassio and stabbing of Roderigo (act 5, scene 1) was also omitted. Rossi did not enter the bedchamber, as Salvini did, with an air of grim determination but quietly and sadly, almost diffidently. The bed was placed up center with its downstage curtains open and upstage ones closed. These were of a rich crimson, with a rosy light playing upon the figure of the sleeping Desdemona. Rossi walked slowly to upstage of the bed and stood over it, like a dark shadow against the curtains, to deliver his opening speech, "It is the cause." He then came around and sat upon the bed for his conversation with the awakened woman. The entire scene was played on the bed, with the pleas and protests of Desdemona gradually increasing Othello's wrath until he seized and strangled her. This was done in full view of the audience and with a brutality that on more than one occasion drew hisses and protests from the audience. Rossi first wrapped Desdemona's long hair about her neck and then, as she screamed in fright and agony, clasped his hands about her neck and dashed her to and fro upon the bed (recalling his treatment of Iago in his wrath). Finally he threw her down and extinguished the last spark of life by pressing pillows upon her head. The scene was variously described as "hideous," "revolting," and "appalling beyond belief."

If Rossi's murder of Desdemona was distinctly more shocking than Salvini's, his suicide was clearly less so. Nevertheless, it was equally in the realistic mode and painful enough to those who desired a certain elevation and dignity in tragic presentation. Henry James characterized it, along with most of the final act, as a reduction to "mere emotional sensibility."[4] Instead of Salvini's scimitar across the throat, Rossi pulled forth a dagger and plunged it into his breast, holding it there as he went through the first spasms of his death agonies, his breath coming in spasmodic gasps. He then fell heavily to the floor, struggled to his feet again and staggered to the bed. There he pulled out the dagger and flung it from him. Half-seated, half-reclining on the bed, he passionately took the dead body in his arms, fondled it a moment, then held the pale face at arm's length as he gave the line "I kiss'd thee ere I killed thee." It was spoken in a tone utterly devoid of theatrical flourish and was judged deeply moving. Most critics called Rossi in these final moments more touching, more sensuous, more human, and more pathetic than Salvini. He then fell dead across the body as Lodovico gave the play's final line: "This did I fear."

14

Rossi's *Romeo and Juliet*

Rossi's Romeo, like his Hamlet, was much more favorably received in America than in London. English reviews generally admitted the existence of many fine touches in his portrayal, but once again he was charged with "mere acting," based on no profound intellectual or emotional grasp of the role. Moreover, his Romeo, like his Hamlet, was simply too remote physically from the traditional English conception of the role to be fully accepted by the critics. Frederick Wedmore wrote in the *Academy*:

> Signor Rossi's endeavor to represent Romeo is, so far as physical qualities are concerned, a gallant struggle and a forlorn hope. Now and again, indeed, he does appear so to identify himself with his part that something of the light of youth comes out on his face, but this, which should be constant, is very rare. In the main the vivacity and elasticity of youth are wanting, and to the English eye their place is not supplied by the peculiar suppleness of trained maturity which Signor Rossi can command. The massive head and portly figure ill accord with anybody's notion of a love-sick boy.[1]

Critics in America tended to feel that, though Rossi in age and physique was far from the traditional image of Romeo, he nevertheless achieved a high degree of believability in the role by his emotional sensitivity and the power of his acting. The *Boston Globe* of 11 October 1881 called him "the very ideal of the lover of Verona," and the *New York Times* was equally unqualified in its enthusiasm:

> no eminent actor upon the stage in our day can touch so deeply the truth and poetry of this character as Signor Rossi does. His Romeo was the personification of effeminate beauty and grace, of languid and languishing sentimentalism; the performance was womanly in its delicacy and sweetness, and it lacked no touch of that fitful emotion which is the very poetry of youth.[2]

Henry James cited this role, despite Rossi's "scandalously mutilated" version of the play, as the one in which the actor gave him the most pleasure:

> The things that trouble us nowadays in *Romeo and Juliet*—the redundancy of protestation, the importunate conceits, the embarrassing frankness—all these fall into their place in the rolling Italian diction, and what one seems to see is not a translation, but a restitution.

"It is singular," James continues, "that Rossi should play best the part that he looks least," but "robust and mature as he is, Rossi does it as a consummate artist; it is impossible to imagine anything more picturesquely tender, more intensely ardent."[3]

The sensitivity and delicacy with which Rossi invested this role were apparently particularly striking when he played it, as he often did in America, in close conjunction with Othello, the most rugged and masculine of his roles. American critics spoke with approval and admiration of the sharp contrast in these characters—the loud and deep voice of Othello versus the soft lutelike tones of Romeo, Othello's heavy tread versus the buoyant walk of Romeo, the simple natural courtliness of the Moor versus the elegant, ornate manner of the Veronese.

Rossi himself, though he clearly sought to give an impression of youthfulness, argued that it was a mistake to see Romeo merely as a lovesick adolescent. Much more important, he was a man "who begins with a knowledge of his incompleteness and seeks to fill it. He is obsessed with his ideal, which he finds in the flesh and then cannot conceive of life without it." In this, Rossi argued, Romeo differed sharply from Othello, whose ideal was lost, and from Hamlet, who suffered from a feeling of incompleteness but discovered no embodiment of his desire.[4]

The version of the play which Rossi used was much condensed, and it placed far more emphasis on Romeo than the original did. Juliet's first scene with the nurse (act 1, scene 3) was omitted, though a bit of its dialogue was added into the ball scene, and scenes 1, 2, and 4 of the first act were collapsed together into a single sequence containing the opening fight, an invitation from Benvolio to Romeo to attend the Capulet ball, and a short conversation between Romeo, Benvolio, and Mercutio (without the Queen Mab speech or Romeo's expressions of misgivings at the end of the fourth scene).

The early part of the ballroom scene was expanded by some dialogue between Paris and Capulet on Juliet and her age with a few lines from the omitted Nurse-Juliet scene to cover the exposition originally provided by that scene. When Romeo saw Juliet, the rest of the party withdrew gradually from the stage and the two lovers were left alone while a minuet continued in a distant room. Before any lines were exchanged the two gazed at each other for some moments in mute admiration, both moving slowly apart and bowing in time to the music of the dance. The entire sequence of Tybalt's protest was cut, and so this pantomime served as a bridge between Romeo's "I ne'er saw true beauty till this night" and his first line directly to Juliet: "If I profane with my unworthiest hand. . . ." Rossi seemed at first so spellbound by this vision that he was hardly aware of his actions. He received Juliet's low obeisance without realizing that he should acknowledge it. He was swept up into the kiss on the lips with such enthusiasm that he seemed no longer a timid and reverential lover, but a bold and gay gallant. Then, lost in the delight of this experience, he was stunned into temporary immobility by Juliet's sudden departure. He left the stage in a daze, impervious to the gibes of Benvolio and Mercutio, who had returned to the scene in time to witness the lovers' first kiss.

The first scene of the second act, containing the two friends' jesting search for Romeo, was cut, so that this act began in the Capulet garden. The balcony scene as performed by Rossi was generally effective, though not one of the more highly praised sequences in the production. In London his Juliet, Signora Cattaneo, tended to draw more favorable comment than he did for her expression of budding passion. Rossi's projection of a more mature lover apparently compromised the scene for many, among them the critic for the *Athenæum:*

> He is not under the spell of that rapture of new life which comes to youth with the first knowledge that it is loved. He kisses with assurance, he is rhetorical in speech, and his passion only manifests its excess by discounting, as it were, in imagination, the happiness in store. Lacking those qualities of juvenility and timorousness which conflict with passion, the balcony scene loses the poetry.[5]

In America Rossi's Juliet, Miss Muldener, was herself charged with artificial and rhetorical delivery, while Rossi's depiction of boyish ardor was usually considered quite convincing. When Romeo first appeared beneath the balcony, Juliet let down a long and delicate scarf, like the hair of Rapunzel, which Rossi embraced and kissed as if it were his mistress herself. Then, when she had bid her lover farewell, Juliet in turn wrapped in embrace the scarf which had received his homage—a piece of business which, one London critic reported, threw the audience into a rapture. Scenes 2 and 6 of the second act, the two scenes in Friar Laurence's cell, were combined, and the act ended with the marriage of the young lovers. Scenes 4 and 5, containing the Nurse's meeting with Romeo and the subsequent dialogue with Juliet, were not presented. "The old garrulous dame is allowed to exhibit neither her physical nor moral infirmities," approvingly observed the *Illustrated London News* of 27 May 1876, though Signora Darè was commended for the care and effect with which she simulated the age and manners of the Nurse in the few opportunities the abbreviated script allowed her.

Rossi continued in the third act to remove those scenes which took place in the Capulet home. Thus the act began with the scene containing Tybalt's death, omitted the following scene between the Nurse and Juliet, retained the next scene in Laurence's cell, omitted the next with the Capulets and Paris, and retained the next in the orchard up to the exit of Romeo. For many observers this act was the peak of Rossi's performance, the most varied in emotion, the most powerful and effective. The *Boston Globe* of 11 October 1881 called the duel with Tybalt a "wonderful scene" in which Romeo seemed to forget all else save the murder of Mercutio in a "magnificent though brief burst of power." The parting scene from Juliet demonstrated high emotion of a strikingly contrasted sort: "Ardent and passionate love could find no better exemplar than Rossi's Romeo in this scene. Every look, every movement was a study." The middle scene, in the Friar's cell, provided Rossi with opportunities to exhibit yet other dimensions of his emotional range. Not all critics approved of the extreme physicality, the wild grovelling and breast-beating with which he began this scene, though such action seems indicated by Romeo's

> Then mightst thou speak, then mightst thou tear thy hair,
> And fall upon the ground as I do now,

or by the Friar's

> Thy tears are womanish; thy wild acts denote
> The unreasonable fury of a beast.

Even the critics who found the beginning of the scene too extreme, however, were won over by the naturalness of Rossi's recovery from it, and the quiet joy with which his face lit up as he placed on his finger the ring sent by his mistress. Another much-admired emotional shift came at the end of this act, as the joy of the lovers modulated into the agony of parting. "Dry sorrow drinks our blood" was apparently taken by Rossi as the key to this scene, and he descended to the orchard pale and shaken with the grief of his loss. The *Academy* warmly approved this scene, but could not resist adding:

> eloquent and impressive as are his gestures of departure,
> they are those of middle life with its protesting fondness
> rather than of exuberant youth. So almost a father might take
> leave of his child. Thus, again and again, throughout the
> performance, we are met with this difficulty of age.[6]

The fourth act, consisting primarily of the arrangements for and carrying out of the false death of Juliet, was much reduced in Rossi's version, and the entire act adjusted to take place in Juliet's chamber. The act began with the latter part of act 3, scene 5 after Romeo's exit, with the entrance of Lady Capulet. The first scene of the traditional fourth act followed, reduced only to the latter part of the scene, after the exit of Paris. Instead of Juliet going to the Friar's cell for this sequence, he appeared in her chamber. When the Friar departed, Capulet returned and Juliet began her speech of repentance from act 4, scene 2. The original was followed fairly closely through the remainder of this scene and the next. Signora Cattaneo was much admired in Juliet's major soliloquy. "Her supernatural terrors," said the *Illustrated London News* of 27 May 1876, "were exhibited with a force and abandon which perfectly electrified the house." The brief scene 4 was cut, so that the Nurse discovered Juliet unconscious soon after she had taken the potion, and this final scene was reduced to a mere twenty lines. On Lady Capulet's "Help, help! Call help!," Capulet and the Friar entered, and the act ended with the lines:

Lady Capulet: Ah, she is dead!
Capulet: Juliet!
Friar: Their grief distracts my heart. Who knows but it may precede a time of peace?

Rossi retained the apothecary scene opening the final act, though he reduced it in length and added a touch of crude humor to it, perhaps seeking to convert it into a sequence suggesting the gravedigger scene in *Hamlet*. The first interchange will give an idea of the style:

Apothecary:	Who calls so loud?
Romeo:	A distressed customer.
Apothecary:	Go to hell!

There is no charity to be given here.

The second scene, between Friar Laurence and Friar John, was eliminated, and the final scene in the churchyard radically reworked after the manner of Garrick. According to Rossi's version, Juliet awakens just after Romeo has given his final line and fallen unconscious, but before he is actually dead. Half-unconscious herself, she wanders from the tomb and into the churchyard, calling out to Friar Laurence and her husband. The dying Romeo, pulling himself painfully to the tomb to die beside his Juliet, finds her gone. Henry James observes:

> this gives Rossi an opportunity for a great stroke of dumb show—the sort of thing in which he decidedly excels. He has staggered away from the tomb while the poison, which he has just drunk, is working, and stands with his back to it as Juliet noiselessly revives and emerges. He returns to it, finds it empty, looks about him, and sees Juliet standing a short distance off, and looking in the dim vault like a spectre. He has been bending over the empty tomb, and his eyes fall upon her as he slowly rises. His movement of solemn terror as he slowly throws up his arms and continues to rise and rise, until, with his whole being dilated, he stands staring and appalled, on tiptoe, is, although it is grotesque in description, very well worth seeing.[7]

The *Athenæum* picks up the description of this climactic sequence thus:

> Mastering by one supreme effort the tortures that rend him, he approaches with awe what he believes the wraith of his mistress, until sight, hearing, and other senses are convinced it is she herself, when he strains her in a rapturous embrace, from which he drops back dead. The manner in which the stage is filled by this picture of Romeo's discovery and consternation shows how profound a mastery of art Signor Rossi possesses.[8]

Juliet then delivered her line recognizing her lover's death by poison and stabbed herself. Almost immediately the Friar and the families arrived. The play contained only eight more lines, expressing the agony of the families and ending with the following summation by the Friar:

> Montagues! Capulets! Look at this sad disaster!
> Well may you mourn, my lords, now wise too late,
> These tragic issues of your mutual hate!

15
Rossi's *Macbeth*

Macbeth was the only Shakespearian play in Rossi's repertoire which he played in London but not in America. It
appears to have been a solid and generally traditional interpretation which did not arouse great enthusiasm among the critics
but which also gained more general approval than most of the
other, somewhat more unconventional characterizations that
he offered. The most detailed British critique of the performance was that by Moy Thomas in the *Academy*. Thomas characterized Rossi's Macbeth as

> the Macbeth which most readers, critical and uncritical, con-
> ceive: brave and fearless till guilty imaginings, the tempta-
> tion to speculate on "fate, freewill, foreknowledge absolute,"
> and, above all, the superstitious tendencies peculiar to the
> Scottish nature and the rude age in which the drama is laid,
> unnerve him.[1]

Although Rossi was never considered to have so imposing a
physical presence as Salvini, the English critics usually found
that there was a robust and rather rough quality in all of his
characters and this, condemned in Romeo and Hamlet, was
seen as an advantage in the vigorous soldier Macbeth. The
Illustrated London News of 12 May 1876 felt that, in this role and
others, Rossi most resembled Edwin Forrest in the material

quality of the interpretation as well as in its great physical force.

Rossi sided with Salvini on the question of whether Macbeth was his own master or under the influence of outside forces. He gained little extra impetus from Lady Macbeth, and so much in accord was his soul with the promptings of the witches that some critics felt these were intended by Rossi to represent projections of his state of mind or spirits summoned up by his own inclinations. The *Athenæum* called them "a machine to which human passion supplies the motive force" and noted that Rossi

> indicated more clearly than any previous actor that absorption of mind which comes of the conviction that you are under demonic influences. His look is that of one under a spell of glamor which weighs upon him, and can only be momentarily dispelled by violent action.[2]

Rossi thus greeted the sisters with much less surprise than Salvini, almost as if he recognized them at once for what they were. With them, as with Duncan, Lady Macbeth, and even Banquo's ghost, Rossi was bold, even defiant, the self-assured and daring warrior. When first meeting the King, Rossi regarded him with a fixed look as if already contemplating his murder and, in the following scene with Lady Macbeth, he took the lead in the plotting, much as Salvini had. So powerful was this impression that Rossi had difficulty introducing the note of hesitation crucial to the soliloquy "If it were done when 'tis done" and here some critics complained that he lacked conviction and was unable to carry the audience with him.

Still, once Rossi had struck the difficult balance of resolution and remorse simultaneously working upon him, he maintained this with considerable skill in the following scenes. His next sequence with Lady Macbeth, and in particular the speech "Bring forth men-children only," was thought quite effective, though less so than in Salvini's interpretation. The dagger soliloquy of the second act was generally praised, and indeed Thomas called it "the most imaginative portion of his performance:"

a very fine point being made of a long pause before the utterance of the famous soliloquy, while the eyes are fixed on air, or wandering, as if following the movements of the shadowy weapon. When he draws the curtain of the door leading to Duncan's chamber, his horror of advancing and frequent faltering upon the threshold indicated with picturesque effect his mental struggles.[3]

The scene immediately following the murder was most notable for Rossi's vocal variety. He used no striking physical devices as Salvini had, but like Salvini he vocally "acted out" the scene in the bedchamber, with the mutterings of the drowsy guards and his own futile attempts to say Amen. He gave the "Sleep no more" in a high, shrill tone which some found thrilling and others lacking the proper solemnity for this imaginary ghostly cry. Henry James felt that this sort of "absurd ventriloquial effects" disfigured the whole scene: "Fancy the distracted chieftain reeling out red-handed from his crime and beginning to give 'imitations.' "[4] Rossi's first significant cuts in the play came in this act—the porter scene and the conversation between Ross and the old man which opens act 2, scene 1.

Rossi retained the latter half of this scene, after Macduff's entrance, but used it to open his third act. The scene then flowed directly into the traditional act 3, scene 1, the farewell of Macbeth to Banquo and the commissioning of the murderers. At the conclusion of this scene Rossi did not leave the stage, but was joined by Lady Macbeth, who introduced the next scene with the line "How now, my lord! why do you keep alone?" The presentation then ran without significant cuts through the banquet scene.

Rossi did not show the same degree of terror as did Salvini upon the appearance of the ghost. He rather followed what one reviewer referred to as the "German" practice of greeting the specter not with fear but with rage at finding that when the brains are out the man is not dead. Rossi challenged the ghost boldly, approaching it upon its first appearance, said Thomas, "as closely as a mesmeric professor in the act of operating upon a patient,"[5] and rushing at it with his naked sword when it had the temerity to appear again. Nor did the ghost suggest any reason for Macbeth to be frightened of him. The *Saturday Review* reported that the spirit on its first appearance walked in and out "like a neglected guest who was delighted to find an empty place, which he could not but leave on seeing that it belonged to some one else who was irritated at his occupying it," and on his second appearance "wandered aimlessly in search of a seat, and, finding none, went away as humbly and quietly as he could."[6]

Rossi ended the scene with a piece of business recalling the terrified start of Salvini at this point, but much less justified in terms of the way the banquet scene as a whole was played. As he retired to his chamber, he trod upon his own mantle, lost his footing, and tumbled to the floor in what Henry James called ironically a "handsome somersault." Then, apparently convinced that this was all the work of the ghost and quaking in terror, he again whipped out his sword. This time it dropped from his trembling fingers and, as he bent to retrieve it, his crown fell off and rolled away also. Rossi made no further attempt to regain either of them, but made his exit backing away from them and pointing to them in horror and loathing. It was a striking ending to the act, but rather confusing for audiences attempting to gain a unified impression of the sometimes bold and sometimes fearful Macbeth.

The final scene of the third act was cut entirely, and the fifth scene, with Hecate's long speech, was shifted to open Rossi's fourth act and to lead directly into Macbeth's encounter with the witches there. Rossi chose to place Macbeth far upstage in this scene, with the phantoms appearing at the front. His supporting actors, however, especially in the procession of kings, were so poorly trained and the stage, in the interest of creating an infernal atmosphere, was kept so dark that most spectators gained little more than an impression of milling confusion. Fortunately Rossi had much more competent actors playing Malcolm, Macduff, and Ross than Salvini had, so that the final scene of the fourth act, dependent upon these lesser characters, was strong and effective. The scene before this, containing the murder of Macduff's family, was, as usual, omitted.

Signora Glech-Pareti, Rossi's Lady Macbeth, drew mixed reactions, depending upon the tolerance of critics for her strong physical delivery. Favorable reviews called her work "passionate," "elevated," and "full of realistic power," particularly praising the intensity of her invocation in the first scene and her calculated courtesy to Duncan and to the guests at the banquet. Negative ones accused her of leaving too little to the spectators' imaginations and found the sleepwalking scene, for example, filled with overly specific indications of her mental and moral sufferings.

For ease in staging, Rossi put together the second and fourth scenes of the fifth act, showing the attacking armies, and then gave the third and fifth scenes, with only minor cuts. He played the concluding scenes with a defiant tone, the tone of "bear-like I must fight the course," which made such scenes as his dismissal of the servant bringing news of the invaders highly impressive, but which diminished the possible pathos of his quieter moments. "I have lived long enough" was, according to Thomas, delivered with an amount of action and vehemence quite out of keeping with the meditative vein of the occasion.[7] This reckless desperation carried over, of course, into the final combat with Macduff, which was considered much more impressive than the resigned, halfhearted struggle of Salvini. Even after his right arm was disabled and his sword dashed from him, he struggled vainly to the last with the dagger held in his left hand. Rossi also provided an ending to the play more in keeping with the intention of the original. In Salvini's version the last line spoken had been "And damn'd be him that first cries 'Hold, enough!'" Rossi cut the dialogue between Malcolm and Siward but played the final sequence where Macduff returns (though without Macbeth's head) to hail Malcolm as the new king of Scotland.

16

The Italian Style

In view of the repeated critical reference to the "Italian," "Latin," or "Southern" style of Ristori, Salvini, and Rossi, it is probably worth stressing that in a number of fundamental ways their approach to Shakespeare did not differ markedly from that employed by their English and American contemporaries. The framework within which the Italian stars produced their new effects was still that of the grand manner generally employed throughout Europe and America in the late nineteenth century. Some attention was given to overall stage composition, but the star totally dominated the production and the play was widely considered merely a machine for the display of the star's physical, vocal, and emotional prowess. There was little regard for the integrity of a text. Lines were freely cut and scenes rearranged, sometimes for ease in staging, more often to give increased emphasis to the leading player. Passages were removed in which the star did not appear, other passages shifted to provide the star with an effective and theatrical end to an act. Not infrequently, the Italians were condemned for this sort of adjustment by critics who suggested or stated that this was a particularly Italian fault, but it was the stock-in-trade of the leading Anglo-Saxon producers of the period, the Irvings and Dalys, as well.

In terms of acting style, perhaps the grand manner showed

itself nowhere more clearly than in the emphasis on making striking "points" during a production. The actors clearly sought and critics duly recorded moments of extreme theatricality, which served as central artistic images for each production. The most famous of all was surely the image of Salvini as Othello with his foot poised to stamp the life from the prostrate Iago, but every production contained similar calculated "points." Salvini's business with the twig as scepter in *King Lear* or the shower of falling papers after the play scene in *Hamlet* are other striking examples. Ristori's dashing of her imaginary infant to the floor, Rossi's dancing on the crushed portrait of Claudius in *Hamlet* or throwing away his crown and dagger in *Macbeth*—every production offered by the Italian actors could provide further illustrations of this sort. And it must be remembered that the "point" was merely the most obvious manifestation of an approach to acting which stressed throughout physical and vocal display and a highly developed technique.

In all such matters the major Italian actors of the period had much in common with the English. What then caused critics to speak so often of a distinct Italian style, and of what did it consist? Two related but somewhat different concerns seem to be implied in such comment, one about the Shakespearian acting tradition, the other about the new phenomenon of realism. The Shakespearian tradition is rarely mentioned directly by the critics, but it is often implied, since it was after all the standard by which new productions of the classics were invariably judged. Although all of the Italian stars had some exposure to the great English-language Shakespearian actors of the time, they could hardly be expected to develop their own work within that tradition as a new English actor would. The frequent comment that one or another role by Rossi or Salvini was "not Shakespearian" usually meant, more accurately, that it did not accord with the English acting tradition of that role. In his letter to the *Times*, Rossi argued powerfully, but vainly, against the assumption that there was one "proper" way to play a role like Hamlet. "I have ever regarded Hamlet as a type of humanity at large," he wrote, whose temperament

may exist under any clime, and is not more a product of
Scandinavia than of Italy, and may be expressed as regards
detail of gesture, facial expression, vocal accent in any way
congenial to the artist's natural mode of conveying emotion.
There are vivacious Northerns and heavy apathetic South-
erns; the point is to seize the character of the man Hamlet
and express it as the artist, whatever his own temperament
may be, would express the emotions incident to such a
character were they his own.[1]

That Rossi was forced to make such a plea for tolerance indicates clearly enough that, even if in technique he may not have
differed greatly from some English or American actors, the
unconventionality of his interpretation made him seem alien
and difficult to accept. Salvini's Othello was really the only
Italian Shakespearian role which did not suffer from this bias,
not because it was more conventional than others, but because
critics were willing to allow a "Southern" interpretation of this
Mediterranean character. Hamlet, on the contrary, was seen as
essentially Anglo-Saxon, or at least Nordic, and thus to be
properly understood and interpreted only by actors of that
background. Salvini's Othello, said Henry James, was

> a study of pure feeling—of passion, with as little as possible
> of that intellectual iridescence which, in a piece of portrai-
> ture, is the sign of Shakespeare's hand, but which, less vis-
> ible, or at any rate less essential, in the Moor of Venice than
> in the other great parts, puts the character much more within
> Salvini's grasp than the study of Hamlet, of Lear, of Mac-
> beth.[2]

Dramatic characters, James asserted, naturally present themselves to the Italian imagination "as embodiments of feeling,
without intellectual complications", which gives the Italian actors a particular advantage in scenes of passion and with
characters like Othello in which intellectual contemplation was
subordinated to emotionality. But James, and most Anglo-
Saxon critics, considered that this visceral approach, despite its
occasional power, put most of Shakespeare quite beyond Italian

comprehension. Twentieth-century interpretation, exemplified in the work of such actors as Burton, Williamson, and Finney, has opened the mainstream of English approach to elements of violence and physicality even in the intellectual, phlegmatic Hamlet, but in the late nineteenth century such an emphasis was sufficiently strange and unexpected to be intolerable to some and to all rather alien and shocking. Such touches as Salvini's method of exchanging rapiers with Laertes and Rossi's forcing of the poisoned goblet on Claudius—both standard in modern productions—were thus roundly condemned as offensively Italianate in the 1880s.

The separation of the Italian actors from the English stage tradition might be considered the negative side of the Italian style, explaining, on the basis of external and geographical considerations, what they were not. More interesting and more basic to understanding their own creative process was what they were, and what they shared as Italian actors of the period. Despite the vagaries of individual taste and the imprecision of descriptive terms in theatre criticism, there was general agreement among those who wrote on the Shakespearian performances of Ristori, Salvini, and Rossi that these three great artists had a clear similarity of style, which many connected with the new approach of "realism." Doubtless this owed much to a significant overlap in their background and training. All three had studied with the great Gustavo Modena, the father of modern acting in Italy, whose watchwords were "truth" and "spontaneity" in acting and who was a pioneer in the change from the old repertory system with its stock characters and rapidly rotating plays to a system which required actors to create fully rounded, minutely studied, and thoroughly rehearsed distinctive new characters in each play. A lengthy article in the *New York Tribune* the summer before Rossi's tour discussed the influence of Modena on his three most famous students. Modena, said this appraisal,

> discarded the desiccated classicism and teapot style of the old school, and breathed the breath of life into whatever he touched. . . . All the pupils of Modena, who have been heard of at all, have exemplified the master's wisdom in one nota-

ble way—they have kept their distinct individuality and advanced in pathways of their own.[3]

In Italy as elsewhere in Europe, the period of development of Ristori, Salvini, and Rossi was the period in which "realism" was a major new concern of the theatre, though in Italy as elsewhere the exact meaning of the term varied with the user. Even the "classic" or "idealistic" tragedies of Alfieri could be approached in the new manner, as Rossi showed in commenting on his interpretation of Alfieri's Orestes:

Orestes is not a myth, Orestes is a man. I wanted blood to run in his veins, his muscles to be covered with flesh, a heart to beat beneath his breast, that in his face be reflected the various feelings of his soul, and that his words be given delicate shadings to correspond precisely to those feelings, that his gestures be subject and complementary to the words, so as to appear natural and nothing more than the unconscious accompaniment of the words and feelings.[4]

The rise of realism in the Italian theatre was by no means confined to actors' reinterpretation of the classics. French dramatic theory and practice was highly influential in Italy and, as successive generations of French dramatists challenged the classic, idealistic theatre, their revolt was echoed south of the Alps. Thus Paolo Giacometti and the authors of the *basso romantico* unashamedly copied Hugo, Dumas, and the masters of French melodrama in subject matter, treatment, and love of spectacular effect. Then as the French theatre, led by Augier and Dumas *fils*, turned toward the drama of contemporary life, the work of Paolo Ferrari and his followers provided similar fare for the theatres of Italy. Ferrari, Giacometti, and their contemporaries were the leading dramatists as Salvini, Ristori, and Rossi came to artistic maturity, and it was to these dramatists that these actors turned for new scripts. Thus the influence of Modena's style and the development of Italian playwriting at this period proved mutually reinforcing. According to Zola, who wrote rapturously about the 1877 tour of Salvini and his company to Paris, both authors and actors in Italy had by then far surpassed the French in developing the kind of realistic drama which Zola himself was seeking.[5]

American and English critics attempting to categorize the "Italian style" and to distinguish it from what native actors in general were doing referred frequently to the greater "realism" of the Italians. The *Chicago Daily Tribune* of 11 January 1874, in speaking of Salvini, said: "Of the school of realists he is the prophet, for he has revealed to us the sweeping, irresistible power of that school." For some critics realism, especially when applied to Shakespearian acting, was a term of condemnation, for others merely a descriptive tag, and for others still an epithet suggesting bold and imaginative experimentation. All, however, recognized it as a phenomenon by no means restricted to foreign artists, even if these provided particularly clear examples. A new style which had first been crystallized in dramas of modern life at mid-century was, a generation later, affecting production of the classics as well, and even Shakespeare was not immune. Some audience members doubtless went to see the Italian actors merely as an oddity, others because Salvini and Ristori in particular were for a time almost obligatory cultural attractions; but there were many who attended hoping to find in these foreign artists a model of how Shakespeare could be revitalized by this fresh approach.

Probably a modern theatre-goer, could he witness one of the great Italian stars, would recognize their power and ability as actors, but would find the term realistic grossly inappropriate. It is important always to remember that the Italian style remained firmly within the parameters of the late-nineteenth-century grand manner, which could contain much subtlety but little of the kind of underplaying we associate with realism today. It is probably easiest to gain something of an understanding of what was meant by Italian "realism" if we view it, as these critics did, in opposition not simply to the Shakespearian tradition of acting, but to the more general tradition which might be called "idealized" or "poetic" in style. When Ristori first challenged Rachel, the opposition could not have been clearer. Rachel was the embodiment of French classicism—passionate, but passionate in a manner rigidly controlled by a long tradition of movement and declamation, in works of highly structured proportion and balance. Ristori's more violent and emotional style was a revelation to Paris, even for those who did not entirely approve. Delacroix, for example, commented with clear ambivalence that Ristori presented scenes of agony "in a very true, but very repulsive manner."[6] Similarly Henry James praises the Italians for "an instinctive sense of the picturesque which is beyond our culture" making them superb in the purely physical but always with a touch of vulgarity.[7] So in Rossi's *Othello*, which James characterizes as an "Italian conception:"

> Rossi is both very bad and very fine; bad where anything like taste and discretion is required, but "all there," and much more than there, in violent passion.[8]

Though the plays of Shakespeare were constantly used by the French romantics in attacking the French classic tradition and though English actors in Paris served as models for actors like Lemaître and Bocage in breaking away from the classic style of interpretation, England had evolved its own tradition, imported to America, which, if less consciously codified than French classicism, nevertheless proved strongly resistant to radically new interpretations. It also had distinctly formal features, consistent to a certain extent from play to play and thus discouraging to any actor seeking to create a new character for a traditional role, particularly one with a strongly emotional element. There was enough of a sameness in the movements of most Shakespearian actors in England and America at this time that critics could refer to such a phenomenon as the "tragic stance" or the "tragic strut." The declamation of the text too had a certain predictability, even though it was less regular than that of the French stage. Under such circumstances, any novelty would cause surprise and, by its very unexpectedness, might strike an audience as more "real" simply by its departure from a familiar theatrical tradition. A characteristic of the Italians' acting which emphasized this effect of unexpectedness was their love of sharp contrasts, which manifested itself in several ways. All of them had highly trained and marvelously flexible voices, with the ability, rare in American or English actors of the period, to fill a large theatre with even a whisper. Each of their roles contained speeches presented as showpieces for their vocal skill, either by modulation through an impressive variety of vocal effects or by striking, abrupt transitions between extremely loud and very quiet, intimate passages.

The same love of contrast could be observed within sequences or between scenes. A typical Rossi production could almost be laid out in terms of alternating loud impassioned scenes and quiet gentle ones. Ristori's rapid shifts between forced gaiety to her guests and anguished glances at Macbeth in the banquet scene showed the same device at work within a smaller compass. The classic, idealized theatre avoided rapid shifts in tone, even though, as the romantics discovered, these were often clearly suggested by Shakespeare himself. Whether or not such shifts were in fact "realistic," the sharp contrasts they provided seemed so to nineteenth-century audiences, especially when these contrasts served to heighten the effect of the extreme emotional states being presented, with roars of passionate rage suddenly giving way to the most intimate of whispers.

Another device which would seem anything but realistic today yet which was clearly a critical part of the Italian style was the tendency of these stars to "act out" their lines both vocally and physically (what is today sometimes called "indicating") to a far greater extent than English-speaking actors. This tendency may have been somewhat exaggerated when the audiences did not understand the language, and it doubtless served as an aid to comprehension. But it served also as a powerful support for the emotional content of the scenes, and a significant part of the "realism" of the Italians seems to have been based on their graphic portrayal of actions no traditional English or American Shakespearian player would consider— Rossi's maniacal dancing in *Hamlet*, Ristori's dashing out of the brains of her imaginary babe, Salvini's ghastly drawing of the scimitar across his throat. Henry James remarked on the "gulf" between this style and anything in the Anglo-American theatre:

Madame Ristori has the fortune to come of the great artistic race—the race in whom the feeling of the picturesque is a common instinct, and the gift of personal expression so ample that, even when quite uncultivated, it begins where our laborious attempts in the same line terminate.[9]

Yet for all the repetition of certain features in the work of these three stars—the sharp contrasts in tone, the graphic physical illustrations, the emotionality, the building to memorable "points"—the last and perhaps most important remark to be made about the Italian style was that it was not at all a style which imposed a kind of similarity on all productions. Modena's expressed goal of a strong actor-identification with each character required a long study of the role and, ideally, a quite distinct new creation in each part. Salvini's lengthy preparations for each new Shakespearian play, Rossi's careful study of Shakespeare, Ristori's detailed analysis of Lady Macbeth—all reflect this concern. One of the things about Salvini which most impressed Stanislavski was the length of time the actor also spent before each performance preparing himself anew emotionally for that particular role.[10] Even those critics who felt Salvini or Rossi unsuited for certain roles would often admit that the actors made a clear and usually successful attempt to differentiate each character completely in terms of voice, bearing, style of walk, and gesture. The Italian style had many striking and praiseworthy features, but perhaps, from the perspective of the actors' achievement and of the long-term development of "realistic" acting, no part of it was more significant than this specific and highly controlled diversity.

Appendix

The English and American Tours of Ristori, Salvini, and Rossi

Ristori

1857

F	July	3	Macbeth	London, Lyceum Theatre
M		6	Macbeth	
W		8	Macbeth	
F		10	Macbeth	
W		22	Macbeth	
W		29	Macbeth	
F	Aug	7	Macbeth	
Tu		11	Macbeth	Liverpool, Royal Theatre
Th		13	Macbeth	Birmingham
Tu		18	Macbeth	Manchester, Princess Theatre
S		29	Macbeth	Dublin, Theatre Royal

1858

W	Jun	16	Macbeth	London, St. James Theatre

1863

M	Jun	29	Macbeth	London, Her Majesty's

W	Jul	17		Macbeth	Liverpool, Royal Theatre
S	Jul	20		Macbeth (act 4)	London, Her Majesty's

1866–67

F	Oct	19		Macbeth	New York, Théâtre Français
M		22		Macbeth	
Th		25		Macbeth	Brooklyn, Brooklyn Academy of Music
S		27	mat	Macbeth	New York, Théâtre Français
Tu	Nov	6		Macbeth	Boston, Boston Theatre
Th		23		Sleepwalking	New York, Théâtre Français
F		30		Macbeth	Baltimore, Holliday St. Theatre
F	Dec	7		Macbeth	Washington, National Theatre
W		19		Macbeth	Philadelphia, Academy of Music
F	Jan	18		Macbeth	Cincinnati, National Theatre
S	Feb	2		Macbeth	St. Louis, De Bar's Theatre
Th		7		Macbeth	Memphis, Greenlaw Theatre
W	Mar	6		Macbeth	New Orleans, New Opera
M		11		Sleepwalking	New Orleans, National
S		16	mat	Macbeth	Mobile, Temperance Hall
F		22		Macbeth	Louisville, Masonic Hall
S		23	mat	Sleepwalking	
F	Apr	5		Macbeth	Chicago, Crosby's Opera
Th		18		Sleepwalking	Utica, N.Y., Utica Opera
Th	May	16		Macbeth	New York, Théâtre Français

1867–68

F	Oct	25		Sleepwalking	Philadelphia, Academy of Music

1873

F	Jun	11	Sleepwalking	London, Drury Lane
F	Jul	3	Macbeth	London, Lyceum
M		6	Macbeth	
S		11	Sleepwalking	
Tu	Oct	28	Sleepwalking (in English)	London, Opera Comique
Th		30	Sleepwalking	
M	Nov	3	Sleepwalking	Liverpool, Alexandra Theatre
Tu		11	Sleepwalking	Manchester, Queen's Theatre

Salvini

1873–74

Tu	Sept	16		Othello	New York, Academy of Music
Th		18		Othello	
W		24		Othello	
Th		25		Othello	
S		27	mat	Othello	
M		29		Othello	Brooklyn, Brooklyn Academy of Music
Th	Oct	2		Hamlet	New York, Academy of Music
S		4	mat	Hamlet	
S		11	mat	Othello	New York, Wallack's Theatre
M		13		Hamlet	Brooklyn, Brooklyn Academy of Music
Th		16		Othello	New York, Wallack's Theatre
Th		23		Othello	
S		25	mat	Hamlet	New York, Lyceum
W		29		Othello	Philadelphia, Academy of Music
S	Nov	1	mat	Othello	

F		7	Othello	
W		12	Othello	Baltimore, Concordia Opera
S		15	Othello	Pittsburgh, Liberty Hall
M		17	Othello	Washington, Wall's Opera
F		21	Othello	Philadelphia, Academy of Music
W		26	Othello	Boston, Boston Theatre
S		29	mat Hamlet	
W	Dec	3	mat Othello	
S		6	Othello	New Haven, Music Hall
M		15	Othello	New York, Academy of Music
S		27	Hamlet	Rochester, Opera House
M		29	Hamlet	Buffalo, Academy of Music
W		31	Hamlet	Detroit, Opera House
F	Jan	2	Hamlet	Toledo, Wheeler's Theatre
W		7	Hamlet	Chicago, McVicker's Theatre
S		10	mat Hamlet	
Th		15	Hamlet	Louisville, Macauley's Theatre (performance cancelled)
F		16	Hamlet	Louisville, Public Library Hall
Tu		20	Othello	Cincinnati, Pike's Opera
S		24	mat Hamlet	
W		28	Othello	St. Louis, De Bar's Theatre
S		31	mat Hamlet	
W	Feb	4	Othello	Chicago, Hooley's Theatre
W		11	Othello	New Orleans, Varietes
F		13	Hamlet	
W		18	Hamlet	
F		20	Othello	
Tu	May	5	Hamlet	Boston, Boston Theatre
Th		7	Othello	
Tu		12	Hamlet	Providence, Providence Opera

F		15		Othello	Hartford, Conn., Robert's Opera
Tu		19		Hamlet	Washington, National Theatre
S		23	mat	Othello	
Tu		26		Hamlet	Richmond, Va., Richmond Theatre
Tu	Jun	2		Hamlet	Philadelphia, Walnut St. Theatre
F		5		Othello	
W		10		Hamlet	New York, Academy of Music
F		12		Othello	
M		22		Othello	

Ristori

1875

Tu	Mar	23		Sleepwalking	New York, Lyceum
F	Apr	2		Sleepwalking	Boston, Boston Theatre
W		7	mat	Sleepwalking	
F		9		Sleepwalking	Hartford, Conn., Robert's Opera
S		10		Sleepwalking	New Haven, Music Hall
Tu		13		Sleepwalking	New York, Lyceum
Th		15		Sleepwalking	Newark, Newark Opera
S		17	mat	Sleepwalking	New York, Lyceum
F		23		Sleepwalking	Philadelphia, Academy of Music
Th		29		Sleepwalking	Baltimore, Academy of Music
F		30		Macbeth	
F	May	14		Sleepwalking	Chicago, McVicker's Theatre
Th		20		Sleepwalking	Cincinnati, Grand Opera
Tu		25		Sleepwalking	St. Louis, Olympic Theatre

W	Jun	16		Sleepwalking	San Francisco, Macguire's New Theatre
F		18		Sleepwalking	

Salvini

1875

Th	Apr	1		Othello	London, Drury Lane
S		3		Othello	
M		5		Othello	
W		7		Othello	
F		9		Othello	
M		12		Othello	
W		14		Othello	
F		16		Othello	
M		19	mat	Othello	
W		21		Othello	
F		23		Othello	
M		26	mat	Othello	
W		28		Othello	
F		30		Othello	
M	May	3	mat	Othello	
W		5		Othello	
M		10	mat	Othello	
F		14		Othello	
W		19		Othello	
F		21		Othello	
M		24	mat	Othello	
W		26		Othello	
F		28		Othello	
M		31	mat	Hamlet	
W	Jun	2		Othello	
F		4		Hamlet	
M		7	mat	Othello	
W		9		Hamlet	
F		11		Othello	
M		14	mat	Hamlet	

W		16		Othello
F		18		Hamlet
M		21	mat	Othello
W		23		Hamlet
F		25		Othello
M		28	mat	Hamlet
W		31		Othello
F	Jul	2		Hamlet
M		5	mat	Othello
W		7		Hamlet
F		9		Othello
W		14		Othello
F		16		Othello

Salvini

1876

M	May	16		Othello	London, Queen's Theatre
W		18		Othello	
F		20		Othello	
M		23		Othello	
W		25		Othello	
F		27		Othello	
S		28	mat	Othello	
Tu		31		Othello	

Remainder of tour: Newcastle, Manchester, Liverpool, Edinburgh, Glasgow, Dublin, Belfast, and Birmingham

Rossi

1876

W	Apr	19		Hamlet	London, Drury Lane
M		24	mat	Hamlet	
W		26		Hamlet	
F		28		Hamlet	
M	May	1	mat	Hamlet	
W		3		King Lear	

F		5		King Lear
M		8	mat	King Lear
W		10		Macbeth
F		12		Macbeth
M		15	mat	Macbeth
W		17		Hamlet
F		19		King Lear
M		22	mat	King Lear
W		24		Romeo and Juliet
F		26		Romeo and Juliet
M		29	mat	Romeo and Juliet
F	Jun	2		Romeo and Juliet
M		5	mat	Romeo and Juliet
W		7		Romeo and Juliet
F		9		King Lear
M		12		Macbeth
W		14		Macbeth
W		21		Scenes from Hamlet, Othello, Romeo and Juliet, The Merchant of Venice

Salvini

1880–81

M	Nov	29	Othello	Philadelphia, Arch St. Theatre
W		31	Hamlet	

S	Dec	4		Othello	
W		8		Othello	
S		11		Othello	
M		13		Othello	New York, Booth's Theatre
W		15		Othello	
F		17		Hamlet	
M		20		Othello	
S		25		Othello	
W		29		Othello	
F		31		Othello	New Haven, Carll's Opera
M	Jan	3		Othello	Boston, Globe Theatre
W		5		Hamlet	
S		8	mat	Othello	
W		12		Othello	
S		15	mat	Othello	
W		19		Othello	Toronto, Grand Opera
F		21		Othello	Cincinnati, Grand Opera
M		24		Othello	
S		29	mat	Othello	
M	Feb	7		Othello	New York, Booth's Theatre
F		10		Macbeth	
M		14	mat	Othello	
Th		17		Othello	Buffalo, St. James Hall
M		21		Othello	Chicago, McVicker's Theatre
W		23		Hamlet	
S		26		Othello	
M		28		Othello	
Th	Mar	3		Macbeth	
S		5	mat	Othello	
M		14		Othello	St. Louis, Pope's Theatre
Th		17		Macbeth	
S		19		Othello	
M		21		Othello	New Orleans, Grand Opera
S		26		Othello	
M		28		Othello	

S	Apr	2	mat	Othello	
M		11		Othello	Philadelphia, Chestnut St. Opera
Th		14		Macbeth	
S		16	mat	Othello	
M		18		Othello	Boston, Globe Theatre
Th		21		Macbeth	
S		23	mat	Othello	
M		25		Othello	
Th		28		Macbeth	
S		30	mat	Macbeth	
W	May	4		Othello	Washington, Ford's Theatre
S		7	mat	Othello	Baltimore, Ford's Opera
M		9		Othello	New York, Academy of Music
W		11		Macbeth	
S		14	mat	Othello	
Tu		17		Othello	Philadelphia, Chestnut St. Theatre

Rossi

1881–82

M	Oct	3		King Lear	Boston, Globe Theatre
Tu		4		King Lear	
W		5		King Lear	
Th		6		Hamlet	
F		7		Hamlet	
S		8	mat	Hamlet	
M		10		Romeo and Juliet	
Tu		11		Romeo and Juliet	
W		12		Othello	
Th		13		Othello	
F		14		Romeo and	

				Juliet	
S		15	mat	Othello	
M		17		Othello	Providence, Low's Opera
Tu		18		Romeo and Juliet	
Th		20		Othello	Hartford, Robert's Opera
F		21		Romeo and Juliet	
S		22		Romeo and Juliet	Worcester, Mass., Music Hall
M		24	mat	Othello	Boston, Boston Museum
Tu		25		Othello	Lowell, Mass., Huntington Hall
Th		27		Othello	Springfield, Mass., Opera House
F		28		Romeo and Juliet	New Haven, Peck's Grand Opera
S		29		Othello	
M		31		Othello	New York, Booth's Theatre
Tu	Nov	1		Romeo and Juliet	
W		2		Othello	
Th		3		Hamlet	
F		4		Romeo and Juliet	
S		5	mat	Othello	
M		7		Hamlet	
Tu		8		Othello	
W		9		Romeo and Juliet	
Th		10		Hamlet	
F		11		King Lear	
S		12	mat	Hamlet	
M		14		Hamlet	Toronto, Grand Opera
Tu		15		Romeo and Juliet	
W		16		Othello	

M		21	Hamlet	Buffalo, St. James Hall
Tu		22	Romeo and Juliet	
W		23	Hamlet	Rochester, Grand Opera
F		25	Hamlet	Syracuse, Grand Opera
S		26	Hamlet	Utica, Utica Opera
M		28	Hamlet	Albany, Leland Opera
Tu		29	Othello	Troy, Troy Opera
W		30	King Lear	Montreal
Th	Dec	1	Hamlet	
F		2	Othello	
S		3	Othello	Albany, Music Hall
M		5	Hamlet	Philadelphia, Chestnut St. Opera
Tu		6	King Lear	
W		7	Romeo and Juliet	
F		9	King Lear	
S		10 mat	Romeo and Juliet	
Tu		13	Othello	
Tu		20	Hamlet	Charleston, Owen's Academy of Music
W		21	King Lear	
F		23	King Lear	Savannah, Savannah Theatre
Tu		27	Hamlet	Atlanta, Opera House
W		28	Othello	
F		30	King Lear	Richmond, Richmond Theatre
S		31	Hamlet	
M	Jan	2	Hamlet	Baltimore, Ford's Theatre
W		4	King Lear	
Th		5	Othello	
M		9	Hamlet	Washington, Ford's Theatre
W		11	King Lear	
Th		12	Othello	

S		14	mat	Romeo and Juliet	
M		16		King Lear	Brooklyn, Brooklyn Academy of Music
Tu		17		King Lear	New York, Academy of Music
Th		19		Hamlet	Brooklyn, Brooklyn Academy of Music
W		25		King Lear	New York, Academy of Music
Th		26		Othello	
F		27		Hamlet	
S		28	mat	Hamlet	
M		30		Hamlet	St. Louis, De Bar's Theatre
W	Feb	1		King Lear	
F		3		Othello	
M		6		Othello	St. Paul, Opera House
Tu		7		King Lear	
W		8		Hamlet	
Th		9		Othello	Minneapolis, Academy of Music
F		10		King Lear	
S		11	mat	Hamlet	
M		13		King Lear	Chicago, McVicker's Theatre
W		15		Hamlet	
F		17		King Lear	
S		18	mat	Romeo and Juliet	
M		20		Othello	
Tu		21		King Lear	
W		22		Hamlet	
Th		23		Othello	
S		25		Othello	
M		27		King Lear	Milwaukee, Grand Opera
Tu		28		Othello	
Th	Mar	2		Othello	Toledo, Wheeler's Theatre
F		3		Othello	Detroit, Whitney's Grand Opera
S		4	mat	Romeo and	

				Juliet	
			eve	King Lear	
F		24		Lear final scene	Philadelphia, Chestnut St. Theatre
S		25		Lear final scene	
Tu	Apr	11		Othello	San Francisco, Baldwin Theatre
W		12		Othello	
Th		13		Hamlet	
F		14		Hamlet	
S		15		Othello	
F		21		King Lear	
S		22	mat	Othello	
			eve	King Lear	

Rossi

1882

M	Jun	12		King Lear	London, Her Majesty's
W		14		King Lear	
Th		15		King Lear	
S		17	mat	King Lear	
			eve	King Lear	

Ristori

1882

M	Jul	3	Macbeth	London, Drury Lane
Tu		4	Macbeth	
W		5	Macbeth	
Th		6	Macbeth	
F		7	Macbeth	
S		8	Macbeth	
M		10	Macbeth	
Tu		11	Macbeth	

W	12	Macbeth
Th	13	Macbeth
S	15	Sleepwalking
Th	27	Sleepwalking
S	29	Sleepwalking

Remainder of tour: Dublin Gaity Theatre, Sept. 25–30; Belfast, Oct. 2–7; Edinburgh Theatre Royal, Oct. 9–14; Glasgow Theatre Royal, Oct. 16–21; Newcastle, Oct. 23–28; Birmingham, Oct. 30–Nov. 4; Manchester, Nov. 6–11; Leeds, Nov. 13–18; Liverpool Alexandra Theatre, Nov. 20–25; Leicester, Nov. 27–29.

Salvini

1882–83

Th	Oct	26		Othello	New York, Fifth Ave. Theatre
S		28		Othello	
W	Nov	1		Othello	
Tu		7		Othello	
Th		9		Othello	
S		11	mat	Othello	
W		15		Othello	Boston, Globe Theatre
S		18	mat	Othello	
Th		23		Othello	Albany, Tweddle Opera
M	Dec	4		Othello	St. Louis, Pope's Theatre
S		9	mat	Othello	
M		11		Othello	Chicago, Grand Opera
W		13		Macbeth	
S		16		Othello	
W		20		Othello	
S		23	mat	Othello	
W		27		Othello	Detroit, Whitney's Grand Opera
M	Jan	1		Othello	Boston, Globe Theatre
W		3		Macbeth	
S		6	mat	Othello	
M		8		Othello	

F		12		King Lear
S		13	mat	King Lear
M		15		Othello	Philadelphia, Chestnut St. Theatre
W		17		King Lear
S		20	mat	Othello
M		22		Othello	Baltimore, Holliday St. Theatre
W		24		King Lear
S		27	mat	Othello
M		29		Othello	Washington, National Theatre
W		31		King Lear
S	Feb	3	mat	Othello
Tu		6		Othello	Brooklyn, Brooklyn Academy of Music
Th		8		King Lear
M		12		King Lear	Philadelphia, Chestnut St. Theatre
W		14		Othello
S		17	mat	King Lear
M		19		Othello	New York, Academy of Music
W		21		King Lear
S		24	mat	Othello
M		26		King Lear
W		28		Othello
S	Mar	3	mat	King Lear
S		10		Othello	Indianapolis, Dickinson's Grand Opera
M		12		King Lear	St. Louis, Pope's Theatre
W		14		Othello
F		16		King Lear
M		19		King Lear	Chicago, Haverly's Theatre
Th		22		Othello
S		24	mat	King Lear
M		26		Othello	Milwaukee, Grand Opera
Th		29		Othello	Cleveland, Euclid Theatre

W	Apr	4	Othello	Philadelphia, Chestnut St. Theatre
W		11	Othello	Boston, Boston Museum
W		18	Othello	New York, Booth's Theatre
W		25	Othello	
S		28	Othello	

Ristori

1883

Sept. 15–Sept. 30: appearances in Bath, Exeter, Torquay, Gloucester, and Cheltenham

M	Oct	1	Macbeth	Edinburgh, Royal Lyceum Theatre
M		8	Macbeth	Glasgow, Theatre Royal
W		10	Macbeth	
Th		18	Macbeth	Birmingham, Prince of Wales
S		27	Macbeth	Manchester, Princess Theatre
W		31	Macbeth	Dublin
M	Nov	5	Macbeth	Liverpool, Alexandra Theatre

Nov. 15–Dec. 10: appearances in Scarborough, York, Sheffield, Manchester, and Edinburgh

Salvini

1884

Th	Feb	28	Othello	London, Covent Garden
S	Mar	1	King Lear	
M		3	Othello	
W		5	King Lear	
S		8	Macbeth	
M		10	Othello	

W		12		Macbeth
S		15		Othello
M		17		Othello
Th		20	mat	Othello
S		22		Othello
Th		27		Othello
M		31		Othello
Th	Apr	3		Hamlet
S		5	mat	Hamlet

Additional performances in Glasgow, Edinburgh, Dublin, Manchester, Belfast, Liverpool, and Birmingham.

Ristori

1884–85

S	Nov	15		Macbeth	Philadelphia, Chestnut St. Theatre
S		22		Macbeth	Chicago, Haverly's Theatre
S	Dec	6	mat	Sleepwalking	Cincinnati, Robinson's Opera
S		20		Sleepwalking	Boston, Boston Theatre
F	Jan	2		Macbeth	New York, Star Theatre
S		3		Sleepwalking	
Th		8		Sleepwalking	Providence, Providence Opera
S		17		Macbeth	Brooklyn, Brooklyn Theatre
S		24		Sleepwalking	Washington, Albaugh's Grand Opera
F		30		Macbeth	Baltimore, Holliday St. Theatre
S		31	mat	Sleepwalking	
F	Feb	13		Macbeth	New Orleans, Bidwell's Academy of Music
S		14		Sleepwalking	
F		20		Macbeth	Memphis, Levbrie's

					Theatre
S	Mar	7		Macbeth	St. Louis, Olympic Theatre
S		14		Macbeth	St. Paul, Grand Opera
Th		19		Sleepwalking	Minneapolis, Grand Opera
S		21		Sleepwalking	Detroit, Whitney's Grand Opera
Th		26		Macbeth	Philadelphia, Chestnut St. Theatre
M		30		Sleepwalking	Milwaukee, Academy
W	Apr	8		Macbeth	Denver, Tabor Grand Opera
M		20		Macbeth	San Francisco, California Theatre
Tu		21		Macbeth	
S		25		Macbeth	
Th	May	7		Macbeth	Brooklyn, Brooklyn Academy of Music
S		9		Macbeth	Philadelphia, Chestnut St. Theatre

Salvini

1885–86

M	Oct	26		Othello	New York, Metropolitan Opera
W		28		King Lear	
S		31	mat	Othello	
W	Nov	4		Othello	
S		7	mat	Othello	
W		11		Coriolanus	
F		13		Coriolanus	
S		14	mat	Coriolanus	
Tu		17		Othello	Philadelphia, Chestnut St. Theatre
S		21	mat	Othello	
Tu		24		Othello	Worcester, Mass.,

					Worcester Theatre
Tu	Dec	1		Othello	Boston, Boston Theatre
Th		3		Coriolanus	
S		5	mat	Coriolanus	
Tu		8		King Lear	
Th		10		Coriolanus	
S		12	mat	Othello	
Tu		15		Othello	Philadelphia, Chestnut St. Theatre
Th		17		Coriolanus	
F		18		Coriolanus	
S		19	mat	Coriolanus	
F		25		Coriolanus	Brooklyn, Brooklyn Academy of Music
S		26	mat	Othello	
Tu		30		Othello	Cleveland, Euclid Theatre
Tu	Jan	5		Othello	Washington, Albaugh's Grand Opera
Th		7		Coriolanus	
S		9	mat	Othello	
Tu		12		Othello	Chicago, McVicker's Theatre
Th		14		Coriolanus	
S		16	mat	Othello	
Tu		19		Othello	
Th		21		Othello	
S		23	mat	King Lear	
Tu		26		Othello	Omaha, Boyd's Opera
Tu	Feb	2		Othello	San Francisco, Baldwin Theatre
S		6	mat	Othello	
Tu		9		King Lear	
S		13	mat	King Lear	
Tu		16		Othello	
Th		18		Coriolanus	
S		20		Othello	
W	Mar	3		Othello	Denver, Tabor Grand Opera
S		13		Othello	Peoria, Grand Theatre

S		20	mat	Othello	Louisville, Macauley's Theatre
Tu		23		King Lear	Cincinnati, Grand Opera
S		27	mat	Othello	
Tu		30		Othello	Minneapolis, Grand Opera
S	Apr	3		Othello	St. Paul, Grand Opera
S		10		Othello	Detroit, Detroit Opera
Tu		13		Othello	Buffalo, Academy
Th		22		Othello	Baltimore, Holliday St. Theatre

Performances with Booth:

M		26		Othello	Brooklyn, Brooklyn Academy of Music
W		28		Othello	
F		30		Hamlet	
S	May	1	mat	Hamlet	
M		3		Othello	Philadelphia, Academy of Music
W		5		Othello	
F		7		Hamlet	
S		8	mat	Othello	
M		10		Othello	Boston, Boston Theatre
W		12		Othello	
F		14		Hamlet	
S		15	mat	Othello	
M		17		Othello	Brooklyn, Brooklyn Academy of Music

Salvini

1889–90

W	Oct	16		Othello	New York, Palmer's Theatre
F		18		Othello	
W		23		Othello	
M		28		Othello	
S	Nov	2	mat	Othello	

M		4		Othello	Boston, Tremont Theatre
F		8		Othello	
W		13		Othello	
M		18		Othello	Providence, Providence Opera
W		27		Othello	Pittsburgh, Grand Opera House
S		30	mat	Othello	
W	Dec	4		Othello	Philadelphia, Broad St. Theatre
S		7	mat	Othello	
W		11		Othello	Baltimore, Holliday St. Theatre
S		14	mat	Othello	
M		16		Othello	Washington, Albaugh's Opera
S		21	mat	Othello	
W		25		Othello	Pittsburgh, Grand Opera House
S		28	mat	Othello	Cleveland, Lyceum Theatre
W	Jan	1		Othello	Columbus, Metropolitan Opera
M		6		Othello	Chicago, Columbia Theatre
S		18	mat	Othello	
Th		23		Othello	Minneapolis, Grand Opera
S	Feb	1		Othello	Kansas City, Coates Opera House
Tu		4		Othello	Buffalo, Star Theatre
Tu		11		Othello	Philadelphia, Chestnut St. Theatre
S		15	mat	Othello	
W		19		Othello	Richmond, Academy of Music
S	Mar	1	mat	Othello	Brooklyn, Amphion Theatre
S		8	mat	Othello	New York, Broadway

Theatre

Tu	11		Othello	
S	15	mat	Othello	
Tu	18		Othello	Boston, Park Theatre
S	22		Othello	
W	26		Othello	
S	29		Othello	

Notes

Chapter 1. Shakespeare Comes to Italy

1. Quoted in Lacy Collison–Morley, *Shakespeare in Italy* (Stratford, 1916), 6–7.
2. Ibid., 19–20.
3. Voltaire, *Théâtre complet* (Geneva, 1768), 2:201–2.
4. Carlo Goldoni, *Tutte le Opere* (Milan, 1935), 5:1059.
5. Ibid., 1019–20.
6. Giuseppe Baretti, *Opere scelte* (Turin, 1972), 1:242–45.
7. Ibid., 2:548.
8. Baretti, *Epistolario* (Bari, 1936), 2:236.
9. Hilary Gatti, *Shakespeare nei teatri Milanesi dell'Ottocento* (Bari, 1968), 32–33.
10. Vincenzo Monti, *Opere* (Milan, 1953), 1003.
11. Leonardo Bragaglia, *Shakespeare in Italia* (Rome, 1973), 18.
12. Vittorio Alfieri, *Vita* (Florence, 1932), 220.
13. Ugo Foscolo, *Epistolario* (Florence, 1953), 3:148.
14. Peter Müller, *Alessandro Pepoli als Gegenspieler Vittorio Alfieri* (Munich, 1974), 201–3.
15. Alessandro Manzoni, *Lettere* (Verona, 1970), 1:157–58.
16. Anna Busi, *Otello in Italia* (Bari, 1973), 151–55.
17. Ernesto Rossi, *Studii drammatici e lettere autobiografiche* (Florence, 1885), 83–85.
18. Gatti, *Shakespeare*, 44–45.
19. Ibid., 51.
20. Pietro Ferrigni, *La morte di una muse* (Florence, 1885), 2:157.
21. Giulio Carcano, *Teatro di Shakespeare* (Naples, 1914), 1.
22. Rossi, *Studii*, 127.
23. Bragaglia, *Shakespeare*, 28.
24. Tommaso Salvini, *Leaves from the Autobiography of Tommaso Salvini* (New York, 1893), 75.

Chapter 2. The Tours of Adelaide Ristori

1. Cristina Giorcelli, "Adelaide Ristori sulle scene britanniche e irlandesi," *Teatro Archivio* 5 (Sept. 1981): 91.

207

2. Adelaide Ristori, *Memoirs and Artistic Studies,* trans. G. Mantellini (New York, 1907), 43.

3. Giorcelli, "Adelaide Ristori," 85.

4. Eugenio Buonaccorsi, "Adelaide Ristori in America, 1866–67," *Teatro Archivio* 5(Sept. 1981): 159.

5. Ibid., 172–75.

6. Ristori, *Memoirs,* 84.

7. Geneviève Ward and R. Whiting, *Both Sides of the Curtain* (London, 1918), 188.

8. Giorcelli, "Adelaide Ristori," 138–42.

Chapter 3. *Ristori's* Macbeth

1. Eugenio Buonaccorsi, "Adelaide Ristori in America," *Teatro Archivio* 5 (Sept. 1981): 161.

2. John Coleman, "Facts and Fancies about Macbeth," *The Gentleman's Magazine* 62 (March, 1889): 232.

3. Adelaide Ristori, *Memoirs and Artistic Studies* (New York, 1907), 165–66.

4. Henry Morley, *The Journal of a London Playgoer* (London, 1866), 187.

5. *Saturday Review,* 11 July 1857, p. 37.

6. Ristori, *Memoirs,* 168.

7. *Saturday Review,* 19 July 1858, p. 636.

8. Morley, *Journal,* 189.

9. *Saturday Review,* 22 July 1857, p. 888.

10. Ristori, *Memoirs,* 170–71.

11. Laura Caretti, "La regia di Lady Macbeth" in Caretti (ed.), *Il teatro del personaggio: Shakespeare sulla scena italiana dell'800* (Rome, 1979), 165.

Chapter 4. *The Tours of Tommaso Salvini*

1. William Michael Rossetti, *Some Reminiscences,* 2 vols. (New York, 1906), 1:189.

2. *Athenæum* no. 1892 (30 Jan. 1864): 157.

3. Quoted in *New York Times,* 24 August 1873.

4. Celso Salvini, *Tommaso Salvini nella storia del teatro e nella vita del sue tempo* (Bologna, 1955), 275.

5. *New York Times,* 24 June 1874.

6. G. H. Lewes, *On Actors and the Art of Acting* (London, 1875), 275.

7. Tommaso Salvini, *Leaves from the Autobiography* (New York, 1892), 170.

8. Robert Speaight, *William Poel and the Elizabethan Revival* (Cambridge, Mass., 1954), 26.

9. Salvini, *Leaves,* 171–73.

10. Ibid., 196–97.

11. Ibid., 201.

12. *Philadelphia Public Ledger,* 30 Nov. 1880.

13. *St. Louis Globe-Democrat,* 15 March 1881.

14. Quoted in the *New Orleans Times-Picayune,* 13 Feb. 1881.

15. Salvini, *Leaves,* 223.

16. *New York Times,* 20 May 1886.

17. Salvini, *Leaves,* 235.

Chapter 5. Salvini's Othello

1. John Rankin Towse also recalls that Salvini's performance "never altered. . . . Every motion and attitude was the result of conscientious study, every representation was an exact reproduction of its predecessor. . . . And yet there was nowhere the least trace of premeditation or suggestion of mechanism." *Sixty Years of the Theatre* (New York, 1916), 165.

2. Henry James, *The Scenic Art* (New York, 1957), 172.

3. *Spectator,* 17 April 1875.

4. *New York World,* 27 Oct. 1885.

5. *Athenæum* no. 1892 (30 Jan. 1864): 157.

6. *New York World,* 27 Oct. 1885.

7. *Boston Globe,* 14 Dec. 1880.

8. James, *Scenic Art,* 174.

9. *Boston Globe,* 27 Nov. 1873.

10. *Athenæum* no. 1892 (30 Jan. 1864): 157.

11. *San Francisco Chronicle,* 7 Feb. 1886.

12. Quoted in the *Chicago Tribune,* 8 Jan. 1874.

13. *Century Magazine* 23, n.s. 1 (1881): 124.

14. G. H. Lewes, *On Actors and the Art of Acting* (London, 1875), 269, 271–72.

15. *New York Times,* 27 Oct. 1889.

16. James, *Scenic Art,* 174.

17. Ibid., 175.

18. *Boston Globe,* 4 Jan. 1881.

19. *Century Magazine* 23, n.s. 1 (1881): 124–25.

Chapter 6. Salvini's Hamlet

1. Tommaso Salvini, *Leaves from the Autobiography* (New York, 1892), 93.

2. William Winter, *Shakespeare on the Stage,* 3 vols. (New York, 1911), 1:412.

3. *Century Magazine* 23, n.s. 1 (1881): 115.

4. Salvini, "My Interpretation of 'Hamlet' " (trans. Dircé St. Cyr), *Putnam's Monthly* vol. 3, no. 3 (Dec. 1907), 352–53.

5. *Saturday Review,* 5 June 1875, 724.

6. G. H. Lewes, *On Actors and the Art of Acting* (London, 1875), 275.

7. *Century Magazine* 23, n.s. 1 (1881): 115.

8. *Saturday Review,* 5 June 1875, 724.

9. *Boston Globe,* 6 May 1874.

10. Salvini, *Leaves,* 170.

11. *Century Magazine* 23, n.s. 1 (1881): 116.

12. Salvini, "My Interpretation," 354.

13. For example in *Century Magazine,* 23, n.s. 1 (1881): 120.

14. Lewes, *On Actors,* 276–77.

15. *Philadelphia Evening Bulletin,* 1 May 1886.

Chapter 7. Salvini's Macbeth

1. *Century Magazine* 23, n.s. 1 (1881): 121.

2. *Chicago Tribune,* 27 Feb. 1881.

3. Henry James, *The Scenic Art* (New York, 1957), 176.

4. *Academy*, 206 (15 April, 1876): 367.

5. *Saturday Review*, 15 March 1884, 345.

6. Ibid.

7. *New York World*, 11 Feb. 1881.

8. John Coleman, "Facts and Fancies about *Macbeth*," *The Gentleman's Magazine* 42 (March, 1889): 227.

9. *Boston Globe*, 22 April 1882.

10. Coleman, "Facts," 228.

11. *Century Magazine* 23, n.s. 1 (1881): 122.

12. Coleman, "Facts," 228.

13. *Academy* 206 (15 April 1876): 367.

Chapter 8. Salvini's King Lear

1. Interview in *New York Times*, 20 Oct. 1882.

2. *Century Magazine* 23, n.s. 1 (1881): 117.

3. Helen Zimmern, "Salvini on Shakespeare," *The Gentleman's Magazine* 256 (1884): 137.

4. Henry James, *The Scenic Art* (New York, 1857), 179.

5. William Winter, *Shakespeare on the Stage*, 3 vols. (New York, 1915), 2:471.

6. James, *Scenic Art*, 179.

7. Tommaso Salvini, "My Interpretation of 'Lear'" (trans. Dircé St. Cyr), *Putnam's Monthly*, vol. 3, no. 4 (Jan. 1908), 467.

8. *Century Magazine* 26, n.s. 4 (1883): 90.

9. Winter, *Shakespeare* 2:472.

10. Salvini, "My Interpretation," 467.

11. Zimmern, "Salvini," 137–38.

12. *Temple Bar* 75 (1885): 73–74.

13. *Chicago Tribune*, 24 Jan. 1886.

14. James, *Scenic Art*, 180.

Chapter 9. Salvini's Coriolanus

1. *New York Times*, 13 Oct. 1885.

2. *New York Times*, 12 Nov. 1885.

3. *Philadelphia Evening Bulletin*, 18 Dec. 1885.

4. *Boston Globe*, 4 Dec. 1885.

5. *Boston Evening Transcript*, 18 Nov. 1885.

6. William Winter, *Shakespeare on the Stage*, 3 vols. (New York, 1916), 3:230.

Chapter 10. The Tours of Ernesto Rossi

1. *Athenæum* no. 2380 (7 June 1873): 737.

2. Ibid., no. 2482 (22 May 1875): 699.

3. *New York Times*, 9 May 1876.

4. P. M. Potter, "Ernesto Rossi," *The Critic* 1 (1881): 286.
5. *Boston Globe*, 18 Oct. 1881.
6. *New York Times*, 17 March 1882.
7. *San Francisco Examiner*, 22 April 1882.
8. *New York Tribune*, 6 Nov. 1881.

Chapter 11. Rossi's **Hamlet**

1. *Pall Mall Budget* 16 (5 May 1876): 14.
2. *Athæneum* no. 2531 (29 April 1876): 609.
3. William Winter, *Shakespeare on the Stage*, 3 vols. (New York, 1911), 1:417.
4. Ibid.
5. *Saturday Review* 23 (29 April 1876): 548.
6. *Pall Mall Budget* 16 (5 May 1876): 15.
7. *New York Tribune*, 6 Nov. 1881.
8. *Academy* 9 (27 April 1876): 420.
9. *Academy* 8 (25 Dec. 1875): 15.
10. *Pall Mall Budget* 16 (5 May 1876): 15.
11. *Saturday Review* 23 (29 April 1876): 548.
12. Ernesto Rossi, *Studii drammatici e Lettere autobiografiche* (Florence, 1885), 306.
13. *Academy* 8 (25 Dec. 1875): 652.
14. *Saturday Review* 23 (29 April 1876): 548.
15. *Academy* 8 (25 Dec. 1875): 653.
16. *New York Herald*, 4 Nov. 1881.
17. Rossi, *Studii*, 305.
18. Ibid., 309.

Chapter 12. Rossi's **King Lear**

1. *New York Times*, 13 Nov. 1881.
2. *Athenæum* no. 2533 (13 May 1876): 676.
3. *Times* (London), 9 May 1876.
4. *Academy* 9 (6 May 1876): 445.
5. *Boston Globe*, 4 Oct. 1881.
6. *Times* (London), 5 May 1876.
7. *St. Louis Globe-Democrat*, 2 Feb. 1882.
8. *Academy* 9 (13 May 1876): 445.
9. William Winter, *Shakespeare on the Stage*, 3 vol. (New York, 1915), 2:466.

Chapter 13. Rossi's **Othello**

1. *New York Herald*, 1 Nov. 1881.
2. Henry James, *The Scenic Art* (New York, 1957), 55.
3. *San Francisco Chronicle*, 10 April 1882.
4. James, *Scenic Art*, 55.

Chapter 14. *Rossi's* Romeo and Juliet

1. *Academy* 9 (3 June 1876): 546.
2. *Boston Globe*, 11 Oct. 1881.
3. Henry James, *The Scenic Art* (New York, 1957), 53–54.
4. Ernesto Rossi, *Studii drammatici e Lettere autobiografiche* (Florence, 1885), 238.
5. *Athenæum* no. 2536 (3 June 1876): 776.
6. *Academy* 9:546.
7. James, *Scenic Art*, 54.
8. *Athenæum* no. 2536:776.

Chapter 15. *Rossi's* Macbeth

1. *Academy* 9 (13 May 1876): 469.
2. *Athenæum* no. 2534 (20 May 1876): 708.
3. *Academy* 9:469.
4. Henry James, *The Scenic Art* (New York, 1957), 47.
5. *Academy* 9:469.
6. *Saturday Review* 41 (20 May 1876): 651.
7. *Academy* 9:469.

Chapter 16. *The Italian Style*

1. *Times* (London), 9 May 1876.
2. Henry James, *The Scenic Art* (New York, 1957), 189.
3. *New York Tribune*, 7 August 1881.
4. Ernesto Rossi, *Quarant'anni di vita*, 2 vols. (Florence, 1887–89), 1:31.
5. Emile Zola, "Le Naturalisme au théâtre," *Oeuvres complètes* 47 (Paris, 1927): 121.
6. Eugène Delacroix, *Journal*, 2 vol. (Paris, 1932), 2:360.
7. James, *Scenic Art*, 47.
8. Ibid., 55.
9. Ibid., 29.
10. Constantin Stanislavski, *My Life in Art*, trans. J. J. Robbins (New York, 1956), 273–74.

Bibliography

"Adelaide Ristori." *Atlantic* 19 (April 1867): 493–501.

Alfieri, Vittorio. *Vita.* Florence: "La Nuova Italia," 1932.

Archer, Frank. *An Actor's Notebooks.* London: Stanley Paul, n.d.

Baretti, Giuseppe. *Epistolario.* Bari: Laterza, 1936.

———. *Opere scelte.* Turin: Classici Italiani, 1972.

Blake, Charles. *An Historical Account of the Providence Stage.* New York: Benjamin Blom, 1971.

Bragaglia, Leonardo. *Shakespeare in Italia.* Rome: Trevi, 1973.

Brown, T. Allston. *A History of the New York Stage.* 3 vols. New York: Benjamin Blom, 1964.

Browning, Robert. *Letters of Robert Browning.* Edited by T. L. Hood. New Haven: Yale University Press, 1933.

Buonaccorsi, Eugenio. "Adelaide Ristori in America, 1866–67." *Teatro Archivio* 5 (Sept. 1981), 156–88.

Busi, Anna. *Othello in Italia.* Bari: Adriatica, 1973.

Carcano, Giulio. *Epistolario.* Milan: Cogliati, 1896.

———. *Shakespeare's Tragedy of Macbeth.* New York: Sanford, Harroun, 1866.

———. *Teatro di Shakespeare.* Naples: Francesco Perrela, 1914.

Caretti, Laura. "La regia di Lady Macbeth," pp. 147–81 in *Il teatro del personaggio,* ed. Laura Caretti. Rome: Bulzoni, 1979.

Clapp, Henry Austin. *Reminiscences of a Dramatic Critic.* Boston: Houghton Mifflin, 1902.

Clapp, John Bouve, and Edwin Francis Edgett. *Players of the Present.* New York: Benjamin Blom, 1971.

Clapp, William Warland. *A Record of the Boston Stage.* New York: Benjamin Blom, 1968.

Coleman, John. "Facts and Fancies about Macbeth." *The Gentleman's Magazine* 62 (March 1889): 226–33.

Collison-Morley, Lacy. *Shakespeare in Italy.* Stratford: Shakespeare Head, 1916.

"Correspondence: Ristori and Salvini." *The Outlook* 73 (4 April 1903): 811–20.

Costetti, Giuseppe. *Il teatro italiana nel 1800.* Rocca San Casciano: L. Cappelli, 1901.

Crinkle, Nym. "Salvini's Samson and Othello." *The Theatre* (19 Oct. 1889), 527–29.

Delacroix, Eugène. *Journal.* Paris: Plon, 1932.

Duranti, Riccardo. "La doppia mediazione di Carcano," pp. 81–113 in *Il teatro del personaggio,* ed. Laura Caretti. Rome: Bulzoni, 1979.

Emanuel, Giovanni. *Rossi o Salvini?* Bologna: Arnaldo Forni, 1880.

Fennema, David. "Tommaso Salvini in America." Ph.D. dissertation, Indiana University, 1979.

Ferrigni, Pietro. *La morte di una muse.* Florence: Fieramosca, 1885.

"Foreign Actors and the English Drama." *Cornhill* 9 (1863): 172–79.

Foscolo, Ugo. *Epistolario.* Florence: Le Monnier, 1953.

Gagey, Edmond M. *The San Francisco Stage: A History.* New York: Columbia University Press, 1958.

Gatti, Hilary. *Shakespeare nei teatri milanesi dell'ottocento.* Bari: Adriatica editrice, 1968.

Giorcelli, Cristina. "Adelaide Ristori sulle scene britanniche e irlandesi." *Teatro Archivio* 5 (Sept. 1981): 81–155.

Grau, Robert. *The Business Man in the Amusement World.* New York: Broadway Publishing, 1910.

———. *Forty Years Observation of Music and the Drama.* New York: Broadway Publishing, 1909.

Goldoni, Carlo. *Tutte le Opere.* Milan: A. Mondadori, 1935–56.

Hapgood, Norma. "Salvini." *Scribner's Magazine* 35 (Feb. 1904): 234–38.

Healey, W. E. "Salvini." *Littell's The Living Age* 5 (1884): 468–74.

Hornblow, Arthur. *A History of the Theatre in America,* vol. 2. Philadelphia: J. B. Lippincott, 1919.

Hughes, Glenn. *A History of the American Theatre.* New York: Samuel French, 1951.

James, Henry. *The Scenic Art.* New York: Hill and Wang, 1957.

Kellogg, Clara. *Memoirs of an American Prima Donna.* New York: G. P. Putnam's Sons, 1913.

Kemble, Fanny. "Salvini's Othello." *Temple Bar* 71 (July 1884): 368–78.

Kendall, John S. *The Golden Age of the New Orleans Theatre.* Baton Rouge: Louisiana State University Press, 1952.

Knepler, Henry. *The Gilded Stage.* New York: William Morrow, 1968.

Lazarus, Emma. "Salvini's 'King Lear.' " *Century* 5 (May 1883): 89–91.

———. "Tommaso Salvini." *Century* 1 (Nov. 1881): 110–17.

Leavitt, M. B. *Fifty Years in Theatrical Management.* New York: Broadway Publishing, 1912.

Lelièvre, Renée. *Le théâtre dramatique Italien en France.* Paris: A. Colin, 1959.

Leslie, Amy. *Some Players.* Chicago: Herbert S. Stone, 1899.

Lewes, George Henry. *On Actors and the Art of Acting.* London: Smith, 1875.

Manzoni, Alessandro. *Lettere,* 3 vols. Verona: A. Mondadori, 1970.

Mapleson, James H. *The Mapleson Memoirs,* vol. 1. New York: Belford, Clarke, 1888.

Matteo, Gino. *Shakespeare's Othello.* Salzburg: Salzburg Studies in English Literature, 1974.

Monti, Vincenzo. *Opere.* Milan: R. Ricciardi, 1953.

Morley, Henry. *The Journal of a London Playgoer.* London: G. Routledge, 1866.

Morris, Clara. *The Life of a Star.* New York: McClure, Phillips, 1906.

———. *Life on the Stage.* Boston: McClure, Phillips, 1901.

———. *Stage Confidences.* Boston: Lothrop, 1902.

———. "Two Great Othellos." *Munsey's Magazine* 40 (Nov. 1909): 271–78.

Müller, Peter. *Alessandro Pepoli als Gegenspieler Vittori Alfieri.* Munich: Wilhelm Fink, 1974.

Odell, George C. D. *Annals of the New York Stage,* vols. 8–14. New York: Columbia University Press, 1931–45.

Ormsbee, Helen. *Backstage with Actors.* New York: Benjamin Blom, 1969.

"Our Foreign and Native Actors." *Nation* 89 (15 April 1909): 391–92.

Pandolfi, Vito. *Antologia del grande attore.* Bari: Laterza, 1954.

———. *Storia Universale del teatro drammatico,* vol. 2. Turin: Unione Tipografico, 1964.

Potter, P. M. "Ernesto Rossi." *The Critic* 1 (1881): 286–88.

Quinn, Arthur Hobson. *A History of the American Drama*, vol. 1. New York: Harper and Brothers, 1927.

Ristori, Adelaide. *Memoirs and Artistic Studies*. Translated by G. Mantellini. New York: Doubleday, Page, 1907.

Robins, Edward. *Twelve Great Actors*. New York: G. P. Putnam's Sons, 1900.

Rosenberg, Marvin. *The Masks of Othello*. Berkeley and Los Angeles: University of California Press, 1961.

Rossetti, William Michael. *Some Reminiscences of William Michael Rossetti*, vol. 1. New York: AMS, 1970.

Rossi, Ernesto. *Quarant'anni di vita artistica*, 3 vols. Florence: L. Niccolai, 1887–89.

———. *Riflessioni sul teatro drammatico italiano*. Livorno: Gazzetta livronese, 1893.

———. *Studii drammatici e lettere autobiografiche*. Florence: Le Monnier, 1885.

Salvini, Celso. *Tommaso Salvini nella storia del teatro Italiano e nella vita del suo tempo*. Bologna: Cappelli, 1955.

Salvini, Tommaso. "Impressions of Shakspeare's 'Lear.'" *Century* 6 (Feb. 1884): 563–66.

———. "Impressions of some Shakspearean Characters." *Century* 1 (Nov. 1881): 117–25.

———. *Leaves from the Autobiography of Tommaso Salvini*. New York: Century, 1893.

———. "My Interpretation of 'Hamlet.'" *Putnam's* 2 (Dec. 1907): 352–56.

———. "My Interpretation of 'Lear.'" *Putnam's* 3 (Jan. 1908): 465–68.

———. "My Interpretation of 'Macbeth.'" *Putnam's* 2 (Nov. 1907): 211–13.

———. "My Interpretation of 'Othello.'" *Putnam's* 2 (Oct. 1907): 23–29.

———. "Open Letters: Salvini's Tribute to Ristori." *Century* 42 (Apr. 1902), 957–58.

———. *Ricordi, aneddoti e impressioni dell'artista Tommaso Salvini*. Milan: Fratelli Dumolard, 1895.

Scott, Clement W. *The Drama of Yesterday and Today*, 2 vols. London: Macmillan, 1899.

Sherman, Robert. *Chicago Stage*, vol. 1. Chicago: Robert Sherman, 1947.

Speaight, Robert. *Shakespeare on the Stage.* Boston: Little, Brown, 1973.

———. *William Poel and the Elizabethan Revival.* London: Heinemann, 1954.

Stanislavski, Constantin. *My Life in Art.* Translated by J. J. Robbins. New York: Meridian, 1956.

Stirling, Edward. *Old Drury Lane,* 2 vols. London: Chatto and Windus, 1881.

Story, William W. *Roba di Roma,* vols. 1 and 2. London: Chapman and Hall, 1863.

Tompkins, Eugene. *History of the Boston Theatre.* Boston: Houghton, Mifflin, 1908.

Towse, John Rankin. *Sixty Years of the Theatre.* New York: Funk and Wagnalls, 1916.

Voltaire. *Théâtre complèt,* 5 vols. Geneva: n.p., 1768.

Ward, Geneviève and Richard Whiting. *Both Sides of the Curtain.* London: Cassell, 1918.

Willard, George O. *History of the Providence Stage.* Providence: Rhode Island News, 1891.

Wingate, Charles. *Shakespeare's Heroes on the Stage.* New York: Thomas Y. Crowell, 1896.

Winter, William. *Shakespeare on the Stage,* 3 vols. New York: Moffat, Yard, 1911, 1915, 1916.

Zimmern, Helen. "Salvini on Shakespeare." *Gentleman's Magazine* 256 (Feb. 1884): 131–41.

———. "Tommaso Salvini: An Intimate Interview." *The Critic* 42 (Nov. 1904): 412–21.

Zola, Emile. *Oeuvres complètes,* 42 vols. Paris: Bernouard, 1927–29.

Newspapers and Periodicals Containing Reviews, Advertisements, and Itineraries

Academy
Albany Argus
Albany Evening Journal
American
Athenæum
Atlantic Monthly
Baltimore Sun
Boston Daily Journal

Boston Evening Transcript
Boston Globe
Boston Herald
Brooklyn Daily Eagle
Buffalo Commercial
Buffalo Morning Express
Burlington (Iowa) *Saturday Evening Post*
Century Magazine
Charleston News and Courier
Chicago Tribune
Cincinnati Commercial Gazette
Cincinnati Enquirer
Cleveland Plain Dealer
Cornhill Magazine
Critic
Denver Times
Detroit Free Press
Dial
Dramatic Mirror
Dramatic Notes
Dubuque Daily Times
Era
Evansville Journal
Farm and Country
Galaxy
Gentleman's Magazine
Harper's Magazine
Hartford Daily Courant
Illustrated London News
Illustrated Sporting and Dramatic News
Indianapolis Daily Sentinel
Indianapolis Journal
Iowa State Register (Des Moines)
Knowledge
Leavenworth (Kansas) *Standard*
Lippincott's Magazine

Littell's Living Age
London Atlas
London Entr'acte
London Observer
London Spectator
(London) *Times*
Louisville Commercial
Louisville Courier-Journal
McClure's Magazine
Macmillan's Magazine
Milwaukee Daily Republican
Milwaukee Journal
Milwaukee Sentinel
Minneapolis Daily Tribune
Mobile Daily Register
Month
Montreal Gazette
Nashville American
Nashville Daily
Nation
National Review
New Haven Evening Register
New Haven Journal-Courier
New Orleans Times-Picayune
New York Clipper
New York Herald
New York Sunday Mercury
New York Times
New York Tribune
Omaha Daily Republican
Pall Mall Budget
Philadelphia Evening Bulletin
Philadelphia Inquirer
Philadelphia Public Ledger
Pittsburg Daily Post
Providence Journal

Putnam's Monthly Magazine
Richmond Daily Dispatch
Rochester Daily Union and Advertiser
Rochester Democrat and Chronicle
St. James's Magazine
St. Louis Globe-Democrat
St. Louis Post-Dispatch
St. Paul Pioneer Press
Salt Lake Herald
Salt Lake Tribune
San Francisco Chronicle
San Francisco Evening Bulletin
Saturday Review
Spectator
Spirit of the Times
Springfield (Mass.) *Republican*
Syracuse Daily Standard
Temple Bar
Theatre
Theatrical Journal
Toledo Blade
Topeka State Journal
Toronto Globe
Utica Daily Observer
Washington Evening Star
Washington Post

Index